# BUENOS AIRES
## ENCOUNTER

BRIDGET GLEESON

Buenos Aires Encounter
Published by Lonely Planet Publications Pty Ltd
ABN 36 005 607 983

Australia    Head Office, Locked Bag 1, Footscray,
             Vic 3011
             ☎ 03 8379 8000, fax 03 8379 8111
             talk2us@lonelyplanet.com.au
USA          150 Linden St, Oakland, CA 94607
             ☎ 510 250 6400
             toll free 800 275 8555
             fax 510 893 8572
             info@lonelyplanet.com
UK           2nd fl, 186 City Rd,
             London EC1V 2NT
             ☎ 020 7106 2100, fax 020 7106 2101
             go@lonelyplanet.co.uk

This 3rd edition of Lonely Planet's Buenos Aires Encounter
guidebook was researched and written by Bridget
Gleeson, who also wrote the 2nd edition. The 1st edition
was written by Lara Dunston and Terry Carter. This
guidebook was commissioned in Lonely Planet's London
office, and produced by the following. Commissioning
Editors Kathleen Munnelly, Catherine Craddock-Carrillo
Coordinating Editor Charlotte Orr Coordinating Car-
tographer Jennifer Johnston Layout Designer Kerri-
anne Southway Assisting Editor Pat Kinsella Senior
Editor Susan Paterson Managing Cartographer
Amanda Sierp Cover Designer Naomi Parker Managing
Editors Liz Heynes, Kirsten Rawlings Managing Layout
Designer Chris Girdler Thanks to Chris Love

10 9 8 7 6 5 4 3 2 1    3rd edition
ISBN 978 1 74179 825 8    Printed in China

# HOW TO USE THIS BOOK
## Colour-Coding & Maps
Colour-coding is used for symbols on maps and in
the text that they relate to (eg all eating venues on
the maps and in the text are given a green knife and
fork symbol). Each neighborhood also gets its own
color, and this is used down the edge of the page
and throughout that neighborhood section.

Shaded yellow areas on the maps denote
'areas of interest' – for their historical significance,
their attractive architecture or their great bars and
restaurants. We encourage you to head to these
areas and just start exploring!

## Prices
Multiple prices listed with reviews (eg $10/5 or
$10/5/20) indicate adult/child, adult/concession
or adult/child/family.

**Send us your feedback** We love to hear from
readers – your comments help make our books better. We read every word you send us, and we always
guarantee that your feedback goes straight to the
appropriate authors. The most useful submissions are
rewarded with a free book. To send us your updates
and find out about Lonely Planet events, newsletters
and travel news visit our award-winning website:
**lonelyplanet.com/contact**.

Note: We may edit, reproduce and incorporate
your comments in Lonely Planet products such as
guidebooks, websites and digital products, so let us
know if you don't want your comments reproduced or
your name acknowledged. For a copy of our privacy
policy visit **lonelyplanet.com/privacy**.

## BRIDGET GLEESON

Though born and raised in the US, Bridget hasn't lived in her native country in years. She studied in Rome, taught English in Prague, worked with children in an impoverished community in Nicaragua, and listened to countless stories of her mother's solo adventures through South America in the '70s, before arriving in Argentina at the start of 2007. While working on her Spanish and taste-testing Malbec, she's contributed travel writing to *Budget Travel,* Mr & Mrs Smith, Tablet Hotels, *Delta Sky* and Afar. She's also co-authored several Lonely Planet titles, including *Brazil 8, Argentina 7, Buenos Aires 6,* and *New York, New Jersey & Pennsylvania 3*. Bridget photographed many of the images in this book. Follow her travel adventures in real time at www.bridgetgleeson.com.

## BRIDGET'S THANKS

Many thanks to the editors and journalists in Buenos Aires who support me and the porteños who educate me. A special thank you to my family members near and far – especially the one who teaches me how to look at the world through an artistic lens, the one who gives up Saturdays to help me research, and the ones who encouraged me to write and travel in the first place.

## THE PHOTOGRAPHER

Terry Carter has photographed several guidebooks for Lonely Planet, including *Buenos Aires*. He loves shooting the architectural mishmash of the city despite being constantly told his camera will get stolen.

**Cover photograph** A couple tango dancing to accordian music in a Buenos Aires cafe, Chad Ehlers. **Internal photographs** p126 by Bridget Gleeson; p143 Marc van der Aa; p114 by Emily Anne Epstein. All other photographs by Lonely Planet Images and by Terry Carter p4, p6, p8, p12, p13, p17, p21, p24, p27, p28, p32, p49, p55, p78, p105, p107, p113, p119, p134, p139, p148; Michael Coyne p15, p20, p140; Michael Taylor p 31; Krzysztof Dydynski p23, p28, p67, p87, p96, p145, p149, p150; Bridget Gleeson p10, p11, p14, p16, p18, p19, p22, p39, p42, p50, p59, p65, p69, p75, p81, p92, p100, p110, p123, p125, p131, p142, p151; Corey Wise p28.

All images are copyright of the photographers unless otherwise indicated. Many of the images in this guide are available for licensing from **Lonely Planet Images:** www.lonelyplanetimages.com

A house in Abasto painted in traditional *filete* (p72) style

# CONTENTS

| | | | |
|---|---|---|---|
| **THE AUTHOR** | **3** | >ART | 147 |
| **THIS IS BUENOS AIRES** | **7** | >SPORTS | 148 |
| **HIGHLIGHTS** | **8** | >ARCHITECTURE | 149 |
| **BUENOS AIRES** | | >BUENOS AIRES | |
| **CALENDAR** | **23** | WITH KIDS | 150 |
| **ITINERARIES** | **27** | **BACKGROUND** | **151** |
| **NEIGHBORHOODS** | **32** | **DIRECTORY** | **160** |
| >MICROCENTRO | 36 | **INDEX** | **170** |
| >PUERTO MADERO | 46 | | |
| >CONGRESO & | | | |
| TRIBUNALES | 52 | | |
| >RETIRO | 62 | | |
| >SAN TELMO | 70 | | |
| >LA BOCA | 84 | | |
| >RECOLETA & BARRIO | | | |
| NORTE | 90 | | |
| >PALERMO | 102 | | |
| >PALERMO VIEJO | 112 | | |
| >LAS CAÑITAS & | | | |
| BELGRANO | 128 | | |
| **SNAPSHOTS** | **134** | | |
| >ACCOMMODATIONS | 136 | | |
| >TANGO | 138 | | |
| >MUSIC | 140 | | |
| >FOOD | 141 | | |
| >BARS | 142 | | |
| >CLUBS | 143 | | |
| >GAY & LESBIAN BA | 144 | | |
| >FASHION | 145 | | |
| >ESTANCIAS | 146 | | |

Why is our travel information the best in the world? It's simple: our authors are passionate, dedicated travelers. They don't take freebies in exchange for positive coverage so you can be sure the advice you're given is impartial. They travel widely to all the popular spots, and off the beaten track. They don't research using just the internet or phone. They discover new places not included in any other guidebook. They personally visit thousands of hotels, restaurants, palaces, trails, galleries, temples and more. They speak with dozens of locals every day to make sure you get the kind of insider knowledge only a local could tell you. They take pride in getting all the details right, and in telling it how it is. Think you can do it? Find out how at **lonelyplanet.com**.

# THIS IS BUENOS AIRES

Buenos Aires runs on nostalgia and cosmopolitan ambition. For every group of trendsetters laughing over cocktails, there's a cluster of old-timers gathered around a radio, a tear rolling down someone's cheek as Carlos Gardel sings of the glowing street lamps of his beloved city.

The dichotomy is rooted in Argentina's stormy past. The capital city, once a prosperous European-style metropolis teeming with glamorous tango halls and grand cafes, has suffered through a military government, inflation and several economic collapses. But somehow Buenos Aires is livelier than ever. A talented generation of designers, soccer players, musicians and restaurateurs have reinvigorated the beleaguered capital, transforming it into one of the most talked-about travel destinations on the planet.

The hype, after all, is warranted – the steak really is the best in the world, dance halls fill with tango students every night of the week, the soccer matches are intense and passionate, and the wine is affordable and delicious. But Buenos Aires' magnetism, as any porteño (BA local) will tell you, extends well beyond such clichés. Architecturally speaking, the city is a fascinating microcosm of styles from colonial to belle epoque to modernist. The Parisian-style cafe circuit, backed by an intriguing literary history, is paradise for bookish types and coffee lovers, and the edgy local fashion scene seduces design-minded travelers.

Gorge yourself on red meat at a rustic *parrilla* (grill restaurant), nurse a bottle of Malbec at an old-fashioned *milonga* (social dance) as local tango dancers embrace dramatically on the wooden dance floor, pull an all-nighter at a thumping electronic venue along the Costanera, revel in gaucho culture at a *peña* (folk music club). Give Buenos Aires some time. Soon you'll begin to understand the bittersweet charm – the poignant collision of old-fashioned sensibility and contemporary revolution – that simultaneously thrills visitors and makes old men shed a tear or two.

**Left** *Hola* from a junior *fútbolista* (soccer player) and friends above the Caminito, La Boca (p86)

| | | |
|---|---|---|
| >1 | Learn to tango in an old-fashioned dance hall | 10 |
| >2 | Honor the dearly departed at the Recoleta Cemetery | 11 |
| >3 | Catch *fútbol* fever at La Bombonera stadium | 12 |
| >4 | Wander the streets of quaint and crumbling San Telmo | 13 |
| >5 | Sip cappuccino at one of the city's classic cafes | 14 |
| >6 | Shop till you drop at the city's open-air fairs | 15 |
| >7 | Taste-test wines from Argentina's best bodegas | 16 |
| >8 | Pay tribute to Las Madres in Plaza de Mayo | 17 |
| >9 | Contemplate fine art and industry at La Boca's Fundación Proa | 18 |
| >10 | Join the hoedown at a country-style *peña* | 19 |
| >11 | Retreat to a leafy urban oasis | 20 |
| >12 | Get down with gauchos | 21 |
| >13 | Dig into juicy steak at a *parrilla* | 22 |

The music at the Feria San Pedro Telmo (p73) will put you in the mood for tango

# >1 MILONGAS

## LEARN TO TANGO IN AN OLD-FASHIONED DANCE HALL

Sensuous and melancholy, the tango is quintessentially porteño (BA local). Though the dance form was born in the brothels of Buenos Aires' poor immigrant barrios, its humble roots are often hidden beneath champagne and glitter at tourist-oriented tango shows. For a more authentic taste of tango, flee the tour-bus masses and dart through the shadows to a *milonga* (social dance). Here you'll find locals of all ages – some in fishnets, others in jeans – acting out human drama and seduction on the dance floor.

Start at Confitería Ideal (p45), a historic downtown cafe with a grand ballroom on the upper level. Antique chandeliers and marble pillars evoke old-world elegance, and the faded velvet and tango orchestras add a certain dusty charm that draws a nightly crowd of experienced local dancers. Classes are held before the *milonga* for the regulars begins at 11pm.

Once you know the difference between Gardel and Piazzolla, take your dancing shoes over to El Beso (p60) or the Centro Region Leonesa (p61; pictured above). Both venues host classes before dimming the lights for a *milonga*. Too shy to wrap your arms (and legs) around a stranger? Just order a glass of wine and watch the city's skilled *tangueros* do their thing. But don't stare too long at the handsome stranger across the room – an open gaze, according to *milonga* etiquette, is an invitation to dance.

For more on tango, see p138.

# >2 CEMENTERIO DE LA RECOLETA

## HONOR THE DEARLY DEPARTED AT THE RECOLETA CEMETERY

Pay your respects to the city's late and great at the spectacular Cementerio de la Recoleta, a necropolis ornate enough to rival Père Lachaise in Paris or the above-ground cities of the dead in New Orleans.

Occupying almost 55,000 sq meters in the center of Recoleta, the cemetery was consecrated in 1882 as Buenos Aires' first public burial ground. Like the surrounding neighborhood, the graveyard quickly grew exclusive – today it's crowded with 4800 tombs holding the remains of the city's most famous families. Among the noteworthy names buried here are 19th-century president Domingo Sarmiento, twice-president Hipólito Yrigoyen, boxing legend Luis Angel Firpo (aka 'the wild bull of the pampas') and, of course, Eva Perón. But don't expect a grandiose monument to the former first lady. Evita's remains are contained in a simple black granite vault in a plot marked by her family name, Duarte.

The appeal of the cemetery goes well beyond the fame of its permanent residents – the intriguing site is a maze of narrow passageways lined with crumbling marble statuary and decorative mausoleums in architectural styles from art nouveau to neo-Gothic. Follow a stray cat through the alleys to discover cherubs in stone relief, stained-glass windows edged with cobwebs, marble angels and bittersweet poetry etched into granite.

See p93 for more information.

HIGHLIGHTS

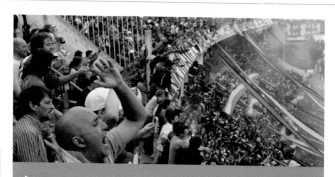

# >3 LA BOMBONERA STADIUM

## CATCH FÚTBOL FEVER AT LA BOMBONERA STADIUM

In Buenos Aires, *fútbol* is not just a game. The national pastime inspires near-religious passion in porteños, clearing the city streets and sending spectators into fits of ecstasy and anguish as they huddle around TV screens or brave the explosive stadium crowds. Witnessing a match at La Bombonera, the famed stadium of Club Atlético Boca Juniors, is an unforgettable experience. But don't brave the volatile masses alone – unless you're going to the game with a streetwise native, it's best to book tickets through a tour operator (see p89).

The city's rival teams symbolize distinct factions of porteño demography. Club Atlético River Plate (known simply as 'River') hails from the affluent north side, while Boca Juniors proudly represents the blue-collar south. La Bombonera, fittingly enough for Boca's home turf, sits smack in the center of one of the city's roughest barrios. Fifty-five thousand frenzied fans take to the stands on Sunday afternoons for two hours of drama; the stadium hums and vibrates as loyal supporters jump in time to rhythmic drum beats and scream at the officials.

The atmosphere is particularly boisterous (read – out of control) when River and Boca face off during the much-anticipated Super-clásico match. Choose between *los millonarios* (the millionaires) and the working-class heroes, then let the games begin – just be sure to dodge the scuffles that inevitably break out in the parking lot.

See also p89.

# >4 SAN TELMO

## WANDER THE STREETS OF QUAINT AND CRUMBLING SAN TELMO

The barrio of San Telmo exudes faded grandeur and bohemian spirit. The neighborhood's elegant belle-epoque architecture and crumbling villas are throwbacks to the district's 19th-century heyday. Before yellow fever and cholera sent the beau monde fleeing for higher ground, aristocratic Spanish families traversed the cobblestone streets in horse-drawn carriages.

After the epidemic, San Telmo's poor immigrants turned abandoned mansions into makeshift homes and the neighborhood quickly fell into disrepair. The pretty barrio has exuded an unpretentious, working-class charm ever since, with antique dealers, tango clubs and restaurants drawing a steady stream of tourists and locals in recent years. The heart of the neighborhood, the Spanish-style Plaza Dorrego (p73), bustles daily with street performers, hippie artisans, beer-swilling backpackers and a clumsy (but occasionally successful) band of local pickpockets.

Wander along Defensa (pictured above) or Balcarce towards the leafy Parque Lezama (p72) and take in the picturesque vista of romantic facades, climbing vines and drooping balconies. After touring El Zanjón de Granados (p72), a colonial mansion that reveals the neighborhood's history, stop into the Mercado de San Telmo (p74) to poke through antique spoons and pick up fresh fruit and cheese for a picnic. Current gentrification efforts may be changing the barrio's character, but the appeal of San Telmo's old-fashioned corner cafes and rustic *parrillas*, thankfully, remains alive and kicking.

See also p70.

# >5 CAFE CULTURE

## SIP CAPPUCCINO AT ONE OF THE CITY'S CLASSIC CAFES

Good news for francophiles, bookworms and travelers who refuse to talk until they've had their morning caffeine jolt: Buenos Aires isn't called the Paris of the south for nothing. In addition to the grand boulevards and art-nouveau architecture that invite comparisons with the French capital, BA's lively cafe culture emanates Parisian appeal.

Once havens for famous writers like Jorge Luis Borges (see p68) and Spanish playwright Federico García Lorca, downtown cafes remain integral to daily life in Buenos Aires. Get your coffee fix with a *café con leche y medialunas* (cafe latte and croissants) and linger in one of the old-fashioned spaces. Here formally dressed waiters serve *porteños* from all walks of life, tango paraphernalia and old photographs cover the walls, and large picture windows frame the activity on busy sidewalks outside.

Embark on a cafe itinerary: start at atmospheric 36 Billares (p59; pictured above), García Lorca's cafe of choice, then move on to Café Tortoni (p43), the city's oldest cafe. Opened in 1858, Tortoni was a regular haunt of the legendary tango singer Carlos Gardel (p56). The flash of tourists' cameras doesn't stop office workers from dropping in for a *cafecito* (small espresso). Ask for a *café cortado* (espresso shot with a little milk) with *churros* (fried, sweet pastries) and absorb the historic atmosphere before finishing the circuit at the stately Café Richmond (p43), the one-time meeting place of Borges and his writer pals.

# >6 ARTISAN FAIRS

**SHOP TILL YOU DROP AT THE CITY'S OPEN-AIR FAIRS**

The sun is shining, the silver is gleaming and pesos are burning a hole in your pocket – there's nothing like an artisan fair on a Sunday morning. On weekends, Buenos Aires' outdoor markets surge with treasure-hunters snapping up everything from antique teapots and Mapuche-inspired silver jewelry to cashmere sweaters and handmade leather boots. Forget economic tensions – this is a shopaholic's playground.

Antique lovers make a beeline for the grandfather of Sunday fairs, the Feria San Pedro Telmo (p73). The main drag, Defensa, throngs with people browsing through cobalt-blue antique seltzer bottles and vintage sunglasses while tango orchestras play in the street (just how did that guy move his piano down his apartment's staircase and across San Telmo's cobblestones?). When the sun sets, an evening *milonga* starts in Plaza Dorrego (p73).

An array of artisan creations from hammered bronze rings to hand-woven leather sandals stock the stalls at the designer market on Recoleta's Plaza Francia (p96; pictured above). Vendors sell sandwiches piled high with slabs of salami and cheese while musical acts play for a barefoot crowd on the grassy slope. Further north, the designer markets skirting Palermo Viejo's Plaza Serrano teem with porteño hipsters scouring the racks for military-style jackets and graphic T-shirts. Don't have much room in your suitcase? Pick up a pair of brightly patterned underthings, a perennial hit with the locals.

See also p145.

# >7 ARGENTINE WINE

### TASTE-TEST WINES FROM ARGENTINA'S BEST BODEGAS

Wine connoisseurs raise their glasses to Argentina, one of the world's premium producers. The industry centers around the Mendoza province, where a sunny, dry climate creates ideal growing conditions; popular grapes include Malbec, which produces a medium-bodied red, and the indigenous Torrontés, the basis for an aromatic white varietal.

Rather than holing up in your hotel room with a bottle of red, appreciate Argentina's impressive wines by attending an educational tasting. Nigel Tollerman, the friendly British proprietor of the wine delivery service 0800-Vino and the sommelier at Francis Ford Coppola's hotel in Buenos Aires, offers casual tastings at his small cellar in Abasto (p108; pictured above). The informal lesson includes an 'aromas kit,' an assortment of cheeses and some hard-to-find special edition wines. More structured tastings with a gourmet food pairing option are run by Anuva Vinos (p130), a wine club that exports carefully selected bottles to the US and Europe. American expat Daniel Karlin conducts tastings at upscale restaurants and, on request, he'll hold a private tasting at your hotel. The poshest wine tasting in Buenos Aires occurs in the elegant cellar at the Alvear Palace Hotel's La Bourgogne restaurant (p98). The knowledgeable sommelier pours varietals and talks tannins while a tuxedoed waiter brings around bite-sized cuisine from the corresponding regions.

# >8 PLAZA DE MAYO

**PAY TRIBUTE TO LAS MADRES IN PLAZA DE MAYO**

Founded in 1580, Plaza de Mayo is a stage on which many of the dramatic events in Argentina's modern history have played out. The central plaza saw massive trade union demonstrations and Eva Perón shouting from Casa Rosada's lower balcony in 1945, military bombings in 1955, and the police shooting of five protestors during the 2001 economic crisis. The pigeon-populated square hosts demonstrations and rallies most days of the week, but the peaceful Thursday vigil of Las Madres de Plaza de Mayo (Mothers of the Plaza de Mayo) is the most powerful and touching.

Since 1977, the Madres have demonstrated against the military-ordered kidnapping, torture and execution of up to 30,000 people during the 1976–83 military government. In memory of their 'disappeared' children and family members, the Madres founded a formal organization to search for the missing, donning symbolic white headscarves and coordinating regular marches demanding justice.

Although in 1986 the Madres split into factions – one focused on locating remains and seeking justice, the other widening their mission to support other causes of injustice – the much-admired mothers came together on April 30, 2007 for a 30th anniversary concert celebrating their courage. Support the cause by stopping by the Madres' bookshop and cafe: Café Literario Osvaldo Bayer (p58).

See also p40.

# >9 LA BOCA

### CONTEMPLATE FINE ART AND INDUSTRY AT LA BOCA'S FUNDACIÓN PROA

You'll do a triple take when you first glimpse the sleek Fundación Proa rising, stately and silver, above the filthy river and broken-down buildings of La Boca. The city's most distinguished art gallery is in fine form after an extensive renovation. Now Proa is a standout, not only for its clout in the international art scene – a Marcel Duchamp exhibit heralded the reopening – but also for its unlikely location in a recycled building on La Boca's gritty riverfront, miles away from the gallery districts of Recoleta and Palermo.

Thanks to Proa and its fashionable terrace cafe, La Boca is again worth a full afternoon's excursion. The barrio, once the city's principal port, owes its vibrant appearance to the Italian immigrants who spruced up their corrugated tin homes with boldly colored paints. Today's tourists swarm Caminito (Little Walkway) and the historic rainbow of houses while professional tango dancers twirl in the street in homage to the dance form that originated here. While the block is visually appealing, it can also feel like a tourist trap filled with second-rate souvenir shops and leather hustlers. Take the obligatory stroll through the historic quarter before you head to Proa, where you can gape at the Riachuelo through the spotless glass panes. Note that the rough-and-tumble barrio has the city's highest crime rate; catch the bus or a taxi back towards the center.

See also p86.

# >10 LA PEÑA DEL COLORADO
## JOIN THE HOEDOWN AT A COUNTRY-STYLE PEÑA

Don't cry into your *cerveza* (beer) if you don't have enough time to spend the day at a country *estancia* (ranch) or visit the suburban Feria de Mataderos (p58) – you can soak up some gaucho culture without leaving the city limits. *Peñas* are folkloric music clubs where regional musicians perform on stage and a jovial crowd chows down on country-style cuisine. After the set, the real festivities commence as the audience passes around harmonicas and *charangos* (five-stringed guitars) for a community jam session.

Rustic, traditional and generally little-known to tourists, *peñas* are scattered about the city. Access the cowboy subculture at Palermo's friendly La Peña del Colorado (p111; pictured above). A country kitchen serves up a full menu of classic dishes from the far reaches of Argentina – Patagonian lamb and *tamales* (steamed cornmeal stuffed with meat and cheese) from the northern province of Tucumán, gnocchi stuffed with cassava grown by the Guaraní tribe – alongside *mate* (a local tea) and Argentine wines. Rotating musical offerings include vocalists from Jujuy province singing old-fashioned laments, Uruguayan guitarists and youthful folk ensembles featuring percussion and wind instruments.

On weekend nights, the *peña* packs in visiting cowboys, gaucho wannabes, eager tourists and stressed-out city dwellers looking to unwind. Get into the mood with free-flowing, sticky sweet *patero* wine – it'll help you work up the courage to grab a harmonica and join the country hoedown at the end of the night.

# >11 CITY PARKS

## RETREAT TO A LEAFY URBAN OASIS

Even the most cosmopolitan traveler needs an occasional escape from the traffic-choked streets of downtown Buenos Aires. Throw together a picnic lunch – a half dozen *empanadas* (savory-filled pastries) and a mini bottle of Malbec should do the trick – and retire to one of the city's green spaces for a lazy afternoon. You'll feel wonderfully indulgent drinking wine on the grass while fitness-conscious *porteños* scamper past in shiny workout garb.

On the north side of the city, the sprawling Parque 3 de Febrero (p107; pictured above) is your best bet for alfresco revelry. The one-time private retreat of 19th-century dictator Juan Manuel de Rosas is now a verdant playground for porteños of all persuasions: families cruising the artificial lake on candy-colored pedal boats, muscled men rolling by on in-line skates, couples kissing in the rose gardens, dreadlocked kids strumming guitars and elderly folk passing around *mate* gourds. For more exotic wildlife, check out the gargantuan koi fish at the nearby Jardín Japonés (p104) and the roaming peacocks at the Jardín Zoológico (p104).

Further south, the Reserva Ecológica (p49) is the riverside refuge of choice. Do as the locals do – pick up a couple of sandwiches, such as a *choripan* (a sausage sandwich) or *bondiola* (piled high with grilled steak) at one of the *parrilla* carts near the entrance, then rent a rusty set of wheels at the adjacent bicycle stand and pedal into the reserve for a picnic near the water.

# >12 LA FERIA DE MATADEROS

## GET DOWN WITH GAUCHOS

Folk music emanates from the outdoor stage, local couples take to the streets to perform the traditional *chacarera* and *chamamé* folk dances, food stalls dish out hearty country dishes like *locro* (a meaty stew from northwest Argentina), deep-fried *empanadas*, and *humitas* (lightly sweetened corn meal wrapped in corn husks), all washed down with sweet *patero* wine – this is La Feria de Mataderos, an authentic celebration of Argentine country traditions.

This lively festival and market is held every weekend (except during the summer) in Mataderos, the western Buenos Aires suburb named for the cattle slaughterhouses established there in 1899. While the stage features children twirling in vibrantly colored skirts and adolescent boys performing gallant folk dances in traditional boots and *bombachas* (loose-fitting gaucho-style trousers), the most exciting spectacle of the day is the *sortija*. In full gaucho regalia, horsemen stand on their saddles and ride at full speed to spear a tiny ring dangling from a ribbon.

After you've marveled at the horses and gorged yourself on country cuisine, stroll through the market for bargain-priced leather goods, ponchos and silver jewelry. A row of gourmet food stands offer samples of homemade cheeses and decadent *dulce de leche* liqueur.

See also p58.

## >13 ARGENTINE BEEF

### DIG INTO JUICY STEAK AT A PARRILLA

Believe the hype: Argentine beef is the best in the world. Eat, drink and be merry at one of Buenos Aires' numerous *parrillas* (grill restaurants), where a leisurely steak dinner begins with waiters pouring Malbec and carving generous slabs of rare prime beef. *Parrillas* run the range from down-to-earth neighborhood joints like La Dorita (p120) and Desnivel (p77), popular spots for inexpensive but traditional grilled specialties, to classic establishments like the refined Don Julio (p120) and stylish steakhouses like Miranda (p121), a favorite of Palermo's fashion-conscious carnivores.

Why is Argentine beef so special? It's the happy cows fattening up on nutritious pampas grass rather than corn and growth hormones. As the meat's primarily produced for export, the leaner, more natural-tasting beef you'll try here is generally not aged, which contributes to its distinct flavor. Another key factor is that Argentine ranchers have kept strict control over breeding, crossing European with British stock to create high-quality and mostly free-range beef.

A *parrillada* (mixed grill) is the meat-eater's litmus test: besides cuts of beef, it almost invariably includes delicacies such as *chinchulines* (intestines), *morcilla* (blood sausage) and *chorizo* (sausage). Sizzling *provoleta* (grilled provolone cheese) and red wine round out the meat-lover's fantasy.

# >BUENOS AIRES CALENDAR

There's always something happening in Buenos Aires. The only time the streets are calm, in fact, is during major *fútbol* (soccer) matches, when locals huddle around their TV sets, and during the sweltering Christmas holidays when half the population decamps to the beach. The cultural calendar has long revolved around traditional pastimes like tango and horses, but the continued growth of the dynamic fine arts scene has brought a host of fashion, music and art events to Buenos Aires' annual schedule. Check out the all-inclusive agenda at www .bue.gov.ar to find out what's on while you're in town.

GERVASI

Carlos Gardel (p56), legendary tango crooner and local hero

# JANUARY & FEBRUARY

## Carnaval

OK, OK, it's a far cry from Rio. But Buenos Aires' Carnaval is fun and lighthearted (though perhaps not for locals stuck in traffic jams as colorful parades shut down a different street every day). Expect to be sprayed with canned foam as ebullient *murga* (dance) troupes dance and drum around Plaza de Mayo.

## Chinese New Year

Buenos Aires' bite-sized Chinatown (p130) only spans a few blocks in Belgrano, but what it lacks in floor space it makes up for with enthusiasm on the first day of the Chinese New Year. Exact dates depend on the lunar calendar.

Nuestros Caballos at La Rural

# MARCH

## Nuestros Caballos

www.nuestroscaballos.com.ar, in Spanish
Argentine horse-lovers gather at Palermo's La Rural (p104) in late March/early April for this all-things-equine exhibition. Expect horse events, produce stalls, and gauchos galore.

# APRIL

## Feria del Libro

www.el-libro.org.ar, in Spanish
Latin American literature is as strong as ever, with over one million book lovers

converging on its most important book fair, featuring book reading and signing sessions by famous authors from around the world.

## Festival Internacional de Cine Independiente

www.bafici.gov.ar, in Spanish
Mid- to late April's excellent independent film festival highlights Argentine, Latin American and international independent films. The main screening venue is at Abasto mall (p108).

# MAY

## arteBA

www.arteba.com
Held over five days in mid-May at Palermo's La Rural (p104), this event features exhibitions

from hundreds of art galleries and organizations in Buenos Aires, with both national and international contemporary art on display, as well as presentations and discussions.

# JUNE

### Día de la Muerte de Carlos Gardel

June 24 marks the anniversary of this iconic tango singer's (p56) death. Numerous tango events during the week conclude with a pilgrimage to the Cementerio de la Chacarita, where thousands of fans, some of whom weren't even born when he died, crowd the streets and leave flowers at his tomb.

# JULY

### La Rural

www.exposicionrural.com.ar, in Spanish
Livestock lovers and gaucho groupies will go crazy at this event in July and August, where prize cows (of course), sheep, goats and horses are on display, along with wild gaucho shows and just about everything agricultural. It takes place at Palermo's La Rural (p104). Gaucho *bombachas* (pants) optional.

# AUGUST

### Fashion Buenos Aires

www.bafweek.com, in Spanish
Rose-colored champagne flows freely, fashionistas chat on iPhones and coltish

teenagers take to the runway – it must be Buenos Aires' biannual fashion week (BAFWeek). For five action-packed days, the finest local designers strut their stuff at Palermo's La Rural (p104).

### Tango Buenos Aires

www.festivaldetango.gob.ar, in Spanish
This tango festival has legs wrapping all over the city. The performances offer a great way to see some of the country's best *tanguistas* (female tango dancers) do their thing. Venues include the Centro Cultural Recoleta (p93).

# SEPTEMBER

### La Semana del Arte en Buenos Aires

www.lasemanadelarte.com.ar, in Spanish
For one week in mid-September, nearly every art gallery and cultural institution in the city opens its doors for a mega-event that highlights some of the best contemporary artists in the country. All forms of media – from photography to video installations and performance art – are represented.

### Feria de Vinos y Bodegas

www.argentinewines.com, in Spanish
This sprawling wine fair sees representatives from 250 bodegas decanting wines and talking shop – heaven for lovers of fine Cabernet.

## Fiesta del Inmigrante

www.fiestadelinmigrante.com.ar

Practically everyone in Buenos Aires is an immigrant – even if once or twice removed. This joyful weeklong festival honors the locals' ambitious ancestors and features ethnic food, music and dance at the Museo de la Inmigración in Puerto Madero (p48).

# OCTOBER

## Casa FOA

www.casafoa.com

This innovative design fair serves two purposes: first, to preserve and renovate a landmark structure, and second, to display the cutting-edge work of local architects, designers and landscapers. The venue changes each year; the festival usually runs from October to December.

# NOVEMBER

## Marcha del Orgullo Gay

www.marchadelorgullo.org.ar, in Spanish

Over 20,000 of BA's gay, lesbian, transgender and bi community march from Plaza de Mayo to the Congreso on the first Saturday

in November, and the colorful party gets bigger each year.

## Creamfields Buenos Aires

www.creamfieldsba.com

Over 60,000 excited dance music fans dance for 16 hours straight (how *do* they manage that, we wonder?) at one of the world's biggest electronic music festivals.

# DECEMBER

## Campeonato Abierto Argentino de Polo

www.aapolo.com, in Spanish

Palermo's dedicated polo arena, Campo Argentino de Polo (p132), is the venue for this, the highlight of the spring polo and people-watching season.

## Christmas & New Year

These holidays are definitely a family affair in Buenos Aires – but 'family-oriented' doesn't necessarily mean 'wholesome' in this case. These are the days of the year when porteños (BA locals) are, believe it or not, likely to drink too much champagne. The illegal fireworks displays at midnight can be a little dangerous – it's best to watch from a rooftop terrace.

The iconic Obelisco (p40) pierces the sky

# ITINERARIES

## ONE DAY

Short on time? Start a marathon day with an alfresco caffeine jolt at La Biela (p99), then venture into the Cementerio de la Recoleta (p93). Take a taxi to elegant Av de Mayo to stare at grand architecture and pop into literary coffeehouse Café Tortoni (p43). Take some obligatory photos at Casa Rosada (p38), then hang a right at Defensa and venture into San Telmo. Tuck into a juicy steak at Gran Parrilla del Plata (p77) and poke through the antiques at Mercado de San Telmo (p74). Watch tango dancers while sitting outside at the historic Bar Plaza Dorrego (p79). Can't get enough tango? Attend a slick dinner show at El Querandí (p83) or observe from the sidelines at a *milonga* (social dance) at Confitería Ideal (p45).

## THREE DAYS

Check the one-day itinerary off your to-do list, then kick off day two at MALBA (p105). Lunch at Freud y Fahler (p120), then shop for stylish threads in the boutiques around Plaza Serrano. Take a coffee break at the New York–style Mark's Deli (p124), then dine with Palermo Viejo's pretty people at Miranda (p121). Switch from big-city cool to country charm with live gaucho music at Peña del Colorado (p111).

On day three, head to La Boca (p84) for art and coffee on the terrace at Fundación Proa (p86). Amble through El Caminito (p86) before returning to Recoleta for lunch at 788 Food Bar (p98) and a stop in the glamorous El Ateneo Grand Splendid bookshop (p95). Stroll down ritzy Av Alvear and take afternoon tea at L'Orangerie (p97) before feasting on fresh fish at Oviedo (p99).

## FIVE DAYS

Put the three-day itinerary behind you before you head over to Puerto Madero to see the antique sailing vessels and Museo Fortabat (p48). Gobble a steak sandwich outside the Ecological Reserve (p49), then pedal towards the river beaches on a rental bike. Go all out for dinner at El Mercado (p50). On day five, pay your respects to Argentina's iconic

---

**Top left** Soul Café (p132) **Top right** Statue in front of Casa Rosada (p38) **Bottom** Jardín Botánico Carlos Thays (p104)

ITINERARIES

> **FORWARD PLANNING**
>
> **Three weeks ahead** A little forethought will make the difference between a pleasant vacation and a cultural experience you'll be talking about for years to come. First, purchase travel insurance and ditch the conspicuous money belt – Buenos Aires' eager pickpockets will snatch it before you know what's hit you. Plan to be in the city during the weekend for San Telmo's antiques fair (p73) and the Feria de Mataderos (p58). Log onto www .whatsupbuenosaires.com, a cool bilingual portal listing cultural happenings from art shows to music festivals, to sign up for event reminders.
>
> **One week ahead** Snap up tickets for musical acts and theatre at www.ticketek.com.ar, and, if you're planning to go to a *fútbol* match, book ahead with a tour operator like **Tangol** (www.tangol.com.ar). This tourist agency also rents out cell phones and laptop computers, to help travelers stay in touch with their parties and make dinner reservations. See p167 for more info on organized tours.

former first lady at Museo Evita (p106) before exploring Palermo Woods (p107) in the afternoon and knocking back a few frozen mojitos at Milión (p99) at night.

## RAINY DAY

Don't blame it on the rain – there's plenty to do in Buenos Aires when the weather turns stormy. Cafe-hop through downtown venues with literary history (p14) and pop into the Museo Xul Solar (p94) before catching an Argentine flick at the Abasto (p108) or Alto Palermo (p107) cinemas. Get lost in the antique stores of San Telmo (see the boxed text, p74) or attend a champagne-soaked opening at an art gallery (see the boxed text, p94). Linger over a rich meal, then settle in for some jazz at cozy Thelonious Club (p111).

## UP ALL NIGHT

This city doesn't sleep. Porteños go out late, stay out late, and rise late. Take a disco nap in the early evening before dining at Gran Bar Danzon (p98) – the busy late-night eatery has a bar where you can continue the party after dessert. Move on to Las Cañitas around midnight for microbrews at Van Koning (p132) or retro cocktails at Soul Café and Supersoul (p132). Hit the clubs after 2am – try cool Niceto Club (p127) or the rollicking venues along the Costanera Norte (p122). Breakfast at Bar 6 (p123) or, on a Sunday, the popular Scandinavian-style brunch at Ølsen (p121).

Tango dancers twirl cheek to cheek in Plaza Dorrego (p73)

## BUDGET BA

Just because you can't afford drinks at the Faena (p51) doesn't mean your vacation's a bust – many of the city's delights are either inexpensive or free. Admission to the art exhibits at Centro Cultural Recoleta (p93) is always free, and MALBA (p105) has half-price tickets on Wednesdays. Tango performances in Plaza Dorrego (p73) or along El Caminito (p86) won't cost you a penny; entrance to parks like the Jardín Botánico (p104) are also gratis. How to dine on the cheap? Look for affordable *menus ejecutivos* (set-lunch menus) or head to a budget-friendly San Telmo steakhouse like Parrilla 1880 (p78). If all else fails, a box of freshly baked *empanadas* (savory-filled pastries) only costs a handful of pesos.

| | | |
|---|---|---|
| >1 | Microcentro | 36 |
| >2 | Puerto Madero | 46 |
| >3 | Congreso & Tribunales | 52 |
| >4 | Retiro | 62 |
| >5 | San Telmo | 70 |
| >6 | La Boca | 84 |
| >7 | Recoleta & Barrio Norte | 90 |
| >8 | Palermo | 102 |
| >9 | Palermo Viejo | 112 |
| >10 | Las Cañitas & Belgrano | 128 |

A day at the office for a dog walker in one of Palermo's parks (p20)

# NEIGHBORHOODS

A grand downtown, a sleek city harbor, a working-class quarter quickly gentrifying, a bohemian enclave turned fashion district – the ever-changing barrios of Buenos Aires are as colorful as a tango dancer's wardrobe and as diverse as the profanities spewed forth by the city's fervent *fútbol* fans.

The urban geography isn't complex if you break it down like the locals do: most porteños (BA locals), consciously or not, divide their hometown into north and south. The former, to generalize, is affluent, clean and contemporary, while the latter is Buenos Aires' historic center and home to the city's most staggeringly beautiful architecture.

But how to decipher this north/south divide? A simple history lesson: the southern neighborhoods were the original stomping grounds of European immigrants who arrived in Buenos Aires at the end of the 18th century. Poor Italians settled near the port of La Boca, and the barrio's been vibrant but run-down ever since. Wealthy Spaniards threw lavish parties and drank wine in the villas of San Telmo until a yellow fever epidemic drove them out of the barrio in 1871. The neighborhood took on a distinct blue-collar feel until recent restoration efforts unveiled the grandeur beneath San Telmo's tattered exterior. Meanwhile, Congreso still features the visually spectacular Av de Mayo, the legacy of creative European architects, and Puerto Madero, the port that once welcomed immigrants into the city, has been redesigned to resemble a stylish London-style harbor.

The rich Spaniards headed north when disease struck San Telmo, and the rest is history. Recoleta became their new outpost – as evidenced by the French-style architecture and aristocrats who still live there today – and you can see money everywhere in the upscale barrios of Palermo Viejo, Belgrano and Las Cañitas. The Microcentro, Buenos Aires' buzzing business district, bridges the gap between north and south. But don't choose between fashion and history – you'll spend plenty of time feasting on red meat and sightseeing on both sides of town.

# >MICROCENTRO

If you suddenly find yourself surrounded by handsome men in spiffy three-piece suits, you'll know you've made it to the Microcentro. The administrative, business and commercial center of the city surges with an energetic crowd during the day – priests filing into the Catedral Metropolitana, investment bankers shouting into their cell phones, free-spirited artisans selling jewelry behind the Cabildo, the Madres marching in protest around the central square and college students highlighting their textbooks in coffee shops. Plaza de Mayo, sitting at the heart of the neighborhood, sees a rally or demonstration almost every day, while traffic-free shopping thoroughfares Florida and Lavalle swarm with on-the-go businessmen and tourists haggling with salesmen over the price of leather jackets. The Microcentro is notoriously hectic, but recent endeavors to pedestrianize more city streets are making the business district more user-friendly – and braving the diverse downtown crowd is all part of the local experience.

## MICROCENTRO

### ◉ SEE

Cabildo de Buenos
  Aires ...........................1 B5
Casa de la Cultura ...........2 B5
Casa Rosada ....................3 C5
Catedral Metropolitana 4 C4
Centro Cultural Borges ..5 B2
Galería Güemes .............6 B4
Iglesia Santa Catalina ...7 B2
Manzana de las Luces ....8 B5
Museo Etnográfico .........9 C5
Obelisco .......................10 A3
Plaza de Mayo .............11 C5

### 🛍 SHOP

Darcos Tango ...............12 A3
Galerías Pacífico .........13 B2

Plata Nativa .................14 B2
Prüne ...........................15 B3
Winery .........................16 B4

### 🍴 EAT

Brasserie Berry ............17 B3
California Burrito
  Company ..................18 C3
Casa Roca ....................19 B3
D'oro ............................20 B5
Pura Vida .....................21 C3
Tomo 1 ........................22 A3

### 🍸 DRINK

Café Richmond .............23 B3
Café Tortoni .................24 A5
La Cigale .....................25 C2

Le Bar ..........................26 C3
New Brighton ..............27 B3

### ⭐ PLAY

Bahrein ........................28 C3
Big One ........................29 A5
Cocoliche .....................30 A5
Confitería Ideal ...........31 A3
Luna Park .....................32 D3
Teatro Gran Rex ...........33 A3

# ◎ SEE

## ◎ CABILDO DE BUENOS AIRES
☎ 4342-6729; Bolívar 65, Microcentro; admission $1; �ržmuseum 11:30am-6pm Tue-Fri, 2-6pm Sat & Sun; Ⓜ Line A Perú, Line D Catedral, Line E Bolívar; ♿

The pristine white Cabildo was the seat of the Spanish-run city government from 1580 to 1821. Today's colonial-style structure is a testament to haphazard city planning: the original Cabildo was supported by 11 arches that spanned Av de Mayo, but six were demolished to make room for new avenues. A small museum inside houses historical artifacts, and on Thursdays and Fridays an artisan fair takes over the courtyard.

## ◎ CASA DE LA CULTURA
☎ 4323-9669; Av de Mayo 575, Microcentro; admission free; ☼ 8am-8pm Mon-Fri, closed Jan; Ⓜ Line A Perú, Line D Catedral, Line E Bolívar

Before the internet, apparently, there was glamour in the newsroom. Step through the huge cast-iron doors of the Casa de la Cultura (Office of Culture) into a vestige of the golden age of newspaper journalism. The lobby's dark-wood kiosks and a display of old-fashioned printing equipment hark back to the days when the building was the headquarters of the daily La Prensa newspaper.

## ◎ CASA ROSADA
☎ 4344-3802; www.museo.gov.ar, in Spanish; Hipólito Yrigoyen 219, Microcentro; admission free; ☼ 10am-6pm Mon-Fri, 2-6pm Sun; Ⓜ Line A Plaza de Mayo, Line D Catedral, Line E Bolívar

Standing before this rosy Renaissance-style palace, you can easily imagine Eva Perón pontificating from the lower balcony. This is the Casa Rosada (Pink House), home to Argentina's presidential offices. Construction began in 1862 on the site of Buenos Aires' fort, and the building was painted pink shortly after. Visitors marvel at the picturesque coral hue without realizing the gritty fact behind it – at the end of the 19th century, ox blood added color and texture to ordinary whitewash.

## ◎ CATEDRAL METROPOLITANA
☎ 4331-2845; cnr Av Rivadavia & San Martín, Microcentro; admission free; ☼ 8am-7pm Mon-Fri, 9am-7:30pm Sat & Sun; Ⓜ Line A Perú, Line D Catedral, Line E Bolívar; ♿

A soaring baroque interior, an eye-catching rococo altar, an intricately tiled floor and a statue of Christ carved from the wood of an algarrobo (carob) tree distinguish the city's main cathedral. The mausoleum is the final resting place of the Liberator General José de San Martín, Argentina's independence leader, and an eternal flame burns outside in his honor.

### CENTRO CULTURAL BORGES

☎ 5555-5359; www.ccborges.org.ar;
Galerías Pacífico, cnr Viamonte & San Martín, Microcentro; admission $15; ⏱ 10am-9pm Mon-Sat, noon-9pm Sun; Ⓜ Line C San Martín, Line C Lavalle; ♿

So, all right, it's in a shopping mall. But this cutting-edge cultural center, named for Argentina's literary giant, hosts major exhibits as well as smaller-scale shows by local artists. And, anyway, it's in a really nice shopping mall – the upscale Galerías Pacífico (p40).

### GALERÍA GÜEMES

Florida 165, Microcentro; ⏱ 8:30am-5:30pm Ⓜ Line B Florida; ♿

The glittering Galería Güemes mall and theater

Here's a fun fact for die-hard fans of *The Little Prince*: Antoine de Saint-Exupéry once lived in an apartment here in the glittering Galería Güemes, now a shopping gallery and theater complex. The French pilot/writer met his wife, an El Salvadorean painter, at a demonstration in the streets of Buenos Aires, and *Night Flight* was based on his experience flying post in South America.

### IGLESIA SANTA CATALINA

cnr Viamonte & San Martín, Microcentro; admission free; ⏱ 8am-6pm, guided tours 3pm Fri; Ⓜ Line C Lavalle

Buenos Aires' first convent, Santa Catalina was founded in 1745 and later occupied by British troops during their second invasion in 1807. Look for the exquisite gilded fixtures and Baroque altarpiece by Spanish carver Isidro Lorea.

### MANZANA DE LAS LUCES

☎ 4342-3964; www.manzanadelasluces .gov.ar, in Spanish; Perú 272, Microcentro; admission free, tours $10-12; ⏱ noon-3pm Tue, Wed & Fri, 3-7pm Sat & Sun; Ⓜ Line A Plaza de Mayo, Line E Bolívar

The Manzana de las Luces (Block of Enlightenment) was once the meeting place of Argentina's intellectual heavyweights. The intriguing complex, connected to nearby buildings by a series of underground tunnels that were rediscovered in 1912, includes a university built by Jesuit missionaries in the early 1700s and the Iglesia de San Ignacio, BA's oldest church.

### ◉ MUSEO ETNOGRÁFICO

☎ 4345-8196; www.museoetnografico.filo.uba.ar; Moreno 350, Montserrat; admission $3-10; ⏱ 1-7pm Mon-Fri, from 3pm Sat & Sun; Ⓜ Line A Plaza de Mayo, Line E Bolívar
Indigenous groups inhabited the region before the arrival of European settlers, and this petite museum pays tribute to the tribes, showing a collection of headdresses, ceramic bowls, decorative masks, cookware, religious relics and tools.

### ◉ OBELISCO

cnr Avs 9 de Julio & Corrientes, Congreso; Ⓜ Line B Carlos Pellegrini, Line D 9 de Julio
Inaugurated in 1936 on the 400th anniversary of the first Spanish settlement and stretching 68m skyward, El Obelisco is more than a point of orientation – love it or hate it, it's a striking symbol of modern Buenos Aires. The monument's popularity peaked in 2005 when it donned a huge pink condom for AIDS awareness day.

### ◉ PLAZA DE MAYO

cnr Avs de Mayo & Bolívar, Microcentro; Ⓜ Line A Plaza de Mayo; Line D Catedral, Line E Bolívar; ♿

Founded in 1580 as the city's first central plaza, Plaza de Mayo is the symbolic and physical center of Argentina's rocky history. The square's name commemorates the May Revolution (1810) that began Argentina's process of independence from Spain. Plaza de Mayo has seen it all – spirited crowds cheering as Evita shouted from the Casa Rosada's (p38) balcony, military bombings in 1955, the march of the Madres as they protest the 'disappearance' of their sons. See also p17.

## 🛍 SHOP

### ▢ DARCOS TANGO

*Souvenirs, Shoes*
☎ 4326-0232; www.darcostango.com; Suipacha 259, Microcentro; ⏱ 10am-8pm Mon-Fri, to 6pm Sat; Ⓜ Line C Diagonal Norte, Line D 9 de Julio
The tango shoes at Darcos aren't called 'magic shoes' for nothing – professional dancers swear by them. This charming little store is located near tango salon Confitería Ideal (p45), convenient if you're looking to trade in your flip-flops for something more glamorous before you hit the dance floor.

### ▢ GALERÍAS PACÍFICO

*Shopping Mall*
☎ 5555-5110; www.progaleriaspacifico.com.ar; cnr Florida & Av Córdoba, Microcentro; ⏱ 10am-9pm Mon-Sat, from noon Sun; Ⓜ Line C San Martín

> Av 9 de Julio – A massive main boulevard, 16 lanes wide – you'll need several minutes just to cross from one side to the other.
> Av Alvear – Recoleta's posh boulevard, thick with ritzy boutiques and luxury hotels.
> Av Corrientes – The city's theater strip, a little Broadway lined with traditional pizzerias and highbrow bookstores.
> Av de Mayo – Grand, historic and architecturally stunning, this elegant avenue is BA's version of the Champs-Elysées.
> Av del Libertador – A busy artery in Recoleta running north–south along the river coast, lined by green parks and historic monuments.
> Av Santa Fe – A stylish but low-key shopping avenue running through Recoleta; also a major transportation route.
> Defensa – The picturesque cobblestoned main street of San Telmo, teeming with student bars, rustic *parrillas* and antique stores.
> Florida and Lavalle – The Microcentro's busy pedestrian thoroughfares. Quick lunch spots, inexpensive cinemas and touristy leather shops.

Built in 1889 by Paris department store Bon Marché, this elegant downtown shopping center contains mostly luxury designer brands. More impressive is the beautiful vaulted ceiling painted by five renowned Argentine artists, including Antonio Berni, and the Centro Cultural Borges (p39) upstairs.

## PLATA NATIVA
*Jewelry, Handicrafts*
☎ 4312-1398; www.platanativa.com; Florida 860, Microcentro; 🕐 10am-6pm Mon-Fri; Ⓜ Line C Lavalle, Line C San Martín
Plata Nativa is owned and operated by a local trio with a passion for South American folk art. Traditional Mapuche Indian designs inspired this collection of burnished silver candelabras, pendants and earrings made with large ruby-red jewels and ethnic oil paintings on fabric.

## PRÜNE
*Leather, Fashion*
☎ 4325-1102; www.prune.com.ar; Florida 481, Microcentro; 🕐 10am-8pm; Ⓜ Line B Florida, Line C Lavalle
The Microcentro's pedestrian thoroughfares are jammed with leather shops and outlets, but Prüne's collection is easily the most sophisticated and contemporary. This downtown branch of the high-end line is one-stop shopping for distressed leather accessories from wide belts to shoulder bags.

### ⌂ **WINERY** *Wine*
☎ 4343-7400; www.winery.com.ar,
in Spanish; Diagonal Roque Saenz Peña
555; ⏰ 9am-9pm Mon-Fri, to 6pm Sat;
Ⓜ Line D Catedral

Bottoms up – you can try before
you buy at Winery. Pay for Argentine varietals by the glass, then snap
up a bottle or two to take home.

## 🍴 EAT

### 🍴 **BRASSERIE BERRY** *French* $$
☎ 4394-5255; Tucumán 775, Microcentro; ⏰ 9am-7pm Mon-Wed, 9am-late
Thu & Fri; Ⓜ Line C Lavalle

With its leather banquettes, classic
French bistro chairs, blackboard
wine lists and rich cuisine, this
brasserie has an authentic Lyon feel.
The place throngs with bankers and
executives at lunch, then takes on
a quieter, more romantic ambiance
when the downtown crowd heads
home for dinner.

### 🍴 **CALIFORNIA BURRITO COMPANY (CBC)** *Mexican* $
☎ 4328-3057; www.cbcburrito.com,
in Spanish; Lavalle 441, Microcentro;
⏰ noon-11pm Mon-Fri; Ⓜ Line B
Florida; 🚌 93, 130, 152; ♿ Ⓥ 👶

Craving guacamole? Pick up a
burrito or a pair of soft-shell tacos
at CBC, a budget-friendly Mexican
fast-food joint opened in BA by
American expats. The open-all-day
taco bar is heaped high with fresh

California Burrito Company

toppings from beef and chicken to
beans and hot *salsa verde*.

### 🍴 **CASA ROCA** *French* $$$
☎ 4393-5777; www.casa-roca.com.ar,
in Spanish; San Martín 579, Microcentro;
⏰ 12:30-4pm Mon-Fri; Ⓜ Line B Florida;
🚌 93, 152

It's not every day that you can take
a lunch break at a 19th-century
Italian-Renaissance mansion. The
onetime home of President General
Roca is now an elegant restaurant
only open for three-course meals at
midday. You'll feel worlds (and cen-
turies) away from the downtown
clamor while dining on roasted
chicken and *pommes frites*.

### 🍴 **D'ORO** *Italian* $$
☎ 4342-6959; www.doro-resto.com.ar;
Perú 159, Microcentro; ⏰ 9am-12:30am
Mon-Fri; 7pm-1am Sat; Ⓜ Line A Perú,
Line E Bolívar; 🚌 22, 24

This tried-and-true Italian wine-bar turns out thin, crispy oven-baked pizzas, mushroom risotto, cappellini tossed with fresh basil and tomatoes, and garlic-topped focaccia bread. A friendly sommelier is on hand to recommend a glass of Cabernet, and atmosphere is busy and pleasantly casual – you'll have to squeeze in sideways at lunch.

### PURA VIDA
*Vegetarian, Organic* $$
☎ 4393-0093; www.puravidajuicebar.com; Reconquista 516, Microcentro; ⏰ 9am-5:30pm; Ⓜ Line B LN Alem; ♿ Ⓥ

Wheatgrass shots, anyone? This sleek and uber-healthy eatery helps counteract the effects of the high cholesterol porteño diet. Try the grilled chicken sandwich with mango and cilantro or the avocado citrus salad – you'll feel less guilty when you're indulging in a steak and a half-liter of Malbec later on.

### TOMO 1
*Modern Argentine* $$$
☎ 4326-6695; www.tomo1.com.ar; Hotel Panamericano, Carlos Pellegrini 521, Microcentro; ⏰ noon-3pm Mon-Fri & 7.30pm-1am Mon-Sat; Ⓜ Line B Carlos Pellegrini; 🚌 10, 17, 29; ♿ 🚹

The decor may be fading, but foodies make a fuss over Tomo 1. Try the *prix fixe* menu and you'll understand why it's considered

one of the city's venerable haute-cuisine temples. Chef sisters Ada and Eve Concaro build the menu around seasonal produce, homemade pasta and fresh fish.

## DRINK

### CAFÉ RICHMOND *Cafe*
☎ 4322-1341; Florida 468, Microcentro; ⏰ 7am-10pm Mon-Sat; Ⓜ Line B Florida, Line C Lavalle; ♿ 🚹

Another favorite of Jorge Luis Borges, the elegant old Café Richmond has been serving afternoon teas (and the great writer's favorite, hot chocolate) since 1917.

### CAFÉ TORTONI *Cafe*
☎ 4342-4328; www.cafetortoni.com.ar, in Spanish; Av de Mayo 829, Microcentro; ⏰ 7:30am-2am Mon-Sat, 9am-1am Sun; Ⓜ Line A Piedras, Line C Av de Mayo; ♿

While tourists tend to outnumber locals at this landmark cafe (the oldest in the country), it still has a special place in the hearts of older porteños nostalgic for the good old days. Tango shows are held in a separate salon most nights at 9:30pm and 11pm.

### LA CIGALE *Bar*
☎ 4312-8275; 25 de Mayo 722, Retiro; ⏰ 6pm-late Mon-Fri, 8pm-late Sat; 🚌 93, 130, 152

La Cigale's wide, curving bar, covered in twilight-blue tiles and

Sentimental types who just can't get enough of Buenos Aires' old-fashioned charms can take a short journey into the city's past by boarding Subte (subway) line A in Plaza de Mayo. The quaint wooden train-cars are the originals from the system's construction in 1913. Ride west to the Castro Barros stop and the breathtaking **Las Violetas** ( ☎ 4958-7387; www.lasvioletas.com; cnr Rivadavia & Medrano), an antique cafe with gorgeous stained-glass windows, polished wood and a bakery turning out Parisian-style bonbons and pastries. The spectacular corner space opened in 1884. Ask for the sampler of exquisite little cakes and sandwiches, served with coffee and freshly squeezed orange juice.

attended by a handful of young cocktail-mixologists, forms the centerpiece of this artistic French-style bar. A few students and twentysomethings filter in early for happy-hour *mojito* specials, but you can barely fit in the door later when themed music nights pull a sizeable crowd.

**LE BAR** *Bar, Dance Club*
☎ 5219-0858; www.lebarbuenosaires .blogspot.com, in Spanish; Tucumán 422, Microcentro; ⏰ noon-2am Mon-Sat; M Line B Florida; ⛿ 93, 152
Provocative design, in-demand DJs, splashy art and killer cocktails – Le Bar is the harbinger of downtown's nightlife Renaissance. The antique four-story building was redone to resemble a fanciful European parlor with tear-drop lamps casting a sexy glow across the jewel-toned interior. Come late to knock back the passion fruit–tinged *Pasiónaria* on the rooftop terrace or in futuristic dug-out seating on the 2nd floor.

**NEW BRIGHTON** *Cafe, Bar*
☎ 4322-1515; www.thenewbrightonsrl. com.ar; Sarmiento 645, Microcentro; ⏰ 8am-late Mon-Sat; M Line B Florida, Line C Sarmiento; ♿ ⛿
A doorman welcomes guests into this beautifully restored landmark where bartenders shake drinks behind a polished wood bar and a pianist tickles the ivories on a baby grand. Order a classic cocktail and elegant hors d'oeuvres.

##  PLAY

**BAHREIN** *Dance Club*
☎ 4315-2403; www.bahreinba.com; Lavalle 345, Microcentro; ⏰ midnight-late Tue-Sat; M Line B Florida, Line C Lavalle; ♿
Stained-glass windows and twinkling chandeliers don't usually work, design-wise, with seventies-style disco balls and modular sofas. But fabulous Bahrein has successfully retained the original fittings of the century-old building while drawing a thoroughly modern

late-night crowd to the 'Funky Room' disco, the electrónica party in the basement, and the laid-back Yellow Bar upstairs.

### ⭐ BIG ONE *Dance Club*

☎ 4334-0097, www.bigone.com.ar; Palacio Alsina, Adolfo Alsina 940, Microcentro; ⏱ 1.30am-late Fri & Sat; Ⓜ Line C Moreno, Line E Belgrano; 🚌 10, 17, 59, 64, 86

On Saturdays, the wrought-iron Palacio Alsina is taken over by a parade of young revelers filing into Big One, the capital's biggest electrónica party. Internationally known DJs keep the sweaty festivities going all night with pumping house and techno; Friday nights (or, rather, Saturday mornings) see an equally huge gay party.

### ⭐ COCOLICHE *Dance Club*

☎ 4331-6413; www.cocoliche.net; Av Rivadavia 878, Microcentro; ⏱ 11pm-late Tue-Sun; Ⓜ Line A Piedras; 🚌 10, 64, 100

This artistic underground club mixes a hipster crowd, and international DJs like Matthew Dear, with a first-class sound system. Show up in the middle of the night to see it at its most happening.

### ⭐ CONFITERÍA IDEAL
*Cafe, Tango*

☎ 5265-8069; www.confiteriaideal.com; Suipacha 380, Microcentro;

⏱ 8am-late Tue-Sun; Ⓜ Line B Carlos Pellegrini, Line C Diagonal Norte, Line D 9 de Julio

Don't judge this downtown institution too quickly – the ground-level cafe is looking worn around the edges, but the upstairs dance hall, with its magnificent domed ceiling and glowing antique lanterns, is straight out of another era – especially when couples are locked together on the dance floor and old tango classics crackle over the loud speakers. See also p10.

### ⭐ LUNA PARK *Concert Venue*

☎ 5279-5279; www.lunapark.com.ar, in Spanish; cnr Bouchard & Av Corrientes, Microcentro; Ⓜ Line B LN Alem

Luna Park is a historic performance venue: Juan Perón met his future wife, the young actress Eva Duarte, at a charity event here. Today this neon-signed classic hosts acts from the Harlem Globetrotters to Alanis Morissette.

### ⭐ TEATRO GRAN REX
*Concert Venue*

☎ 4322-8000; Av Corrientes 857, Microcentro; Ⓜ Line B Carlos Pellegrini, Line C Diagonal Norte, Line D 9 de Julio

Everyone from Björk to Caetano Veloso has taken the stage at this classic theater and musical venue. Book a comfortable seat on the mezzanine level for the choicest view.

# >PUERTO MADERO

Contemporary and squeaky clean, Puerto Madero isn't exactly bursting with local flavor – but it reveals a great deal about local aspirations. Porteños (BA locals) are fiercely proud of the dockside regeneration project that turned this old port into a prosperous commercial zone reminiscent of a London-style city harbor. The original Puerto Madero, located to the east of Plaza de Mayo, was the first sight glimpsed by European immigrants as they arrived in Buenos Aires. The port was abandoned at the end of the 19th century and left alone until ambitious developers kicked off a large-scale renovation of the area in the 1990s, cleaning up the dikes and ripping out rotting boards from the warehouses. Today, the red brick buildings house upscale restaurants, loft apartments and offices, a university and a handful of museums. The most impressive restoration effort was the brainchild of fashion-minded entrepreneur Alan Faena, who commissioned French designer Philippe Starck to help transform an old silo into the fabulous Faena Hotel + Universe in 2005. Further east, shaded bike paths traverse the expansive Reserva Ecológica Costanera Sur (ecological reserve). Take a siesta under the trees before strolling to Puerto Madero at sunset – the historic sailing vessels and ritzy party boats that bob in the water cut a striking silhouette against the flame-colored sunset.

## PUERTO MADERO

### ◎ SEE
El Museo Fortabat .........1  A2
Museo de la
  Inmigración .................2  A1
Museo Fragata
  Sarmiento ...................3  A4
Puente de la Mujer ......4  A3
Reserva Ecológica
  Costanera Sur ............5  C3

### 🍴 EAT
Cabaña Las Lilas .........6  A3
El Mercado ..................7  B4
i Fresh Market .............8  A4
La Parolaccia
  del Mare ...................9  A4

### ⭐ PLAY
Asia de Cuba ..............12  A3
Puro Remo ..................13  A2

### ▼ DRINK
The Library Lounge ...10  B4
White Bar ..................11  B5

#  SEE

## EL MUSEO FORTABAT

☎ 4310-6600; www.coleccionfortabat
.org.ar; Olga Cossettini 141, Puerto Madero Este; admission $15; ⏲ noon-9pm
Tue-Fri, 10am-9pm Sat & Sun; Ⓜ Line B
LN Alem; ♿

You have to hand it to an octo-
genarian who's also a millionaire,
a businesswoman, and the proud
owner of masterpieces by Andy
Warhol and Marc Chagall. This
sleek, newly opened dockside museum showcases the extraordinary
art collection of Amalia Lacroze de
Fortabat, including works by Salvador Dalí, Gustav Klimt, Auguste
Rodin and national visionaries like
Xul Solar and Clorindo Testa.

## MUSEO DE LA INMIGRACIÓN

☎ 4317-0285; Av Antártida Argentina
1355, Puerto Madero; admission by donation; ⏲ 10am-5pm Mon-Fri, 11am-6pm
Sat & Sun; 🚌 6, 20

Old photographs and artifacts
tell the stories of European immigrants who arrived in Buenos
Aires in the late 1880s. Temporarily
closed at time of writing.

## MUSEO FRAGATA SARMIENTO

☎ 4334-9386; Av Alicia Moreau de Justo
900, Dique 3, Puerto Madero; admission
$2; ⏲ 9am-8pm; Ⓜ Line B LN Alem

This elegant former naval ship
has a storied past – it sailed
around the world 40 times
between 1899 and 1938 before
serving as a training school for
Argentina's navy. Hop aboard to
check out the antique nautical
gadgets.

## PUENTE DE LA MUJER

Dique 3, Puerto Madero; Ⓜ Line B LN
Alem; ♿

Puerto Madero is femme-friendly:
all the streets in the neighborhood are named after famous
ladies, and the striking Puente de
la Mujer (Bridge of the Woman) is
the barrio's signature monument.
Unveiled in 2001, the stunningly

### ROW YOUR BOAT ASHORE

Due to water pollution near the city
center, most of the aquatic activity on
the Río de la Plata occurs in the coastal
northern suburbs. But a couple of kayak
outfitters are attempting to bring some
recreation back to the urban waters.
Stroll down to **Puro Remo** ( ☎ 6397-
3545; www.puroremo.com.ar, in Spanish; cnr Juana Manso & Victoria Ocampo)
at Puerto Madero's Yacht Club to look
into your paddling and rowing options.
Offering kayak rental, guided tours and
clean, efficient facilities, the business
also runs longer trips including *asados*
(barbecues) and island excursions in the
Tigre river delta.

Stroll across the Puente de la Mujer

contemporary gleaming-white structure was designed by acclaimed Spanish architect Santiago Calatreva and represents – what else? – a couple dancing the tango.

### RESERVA ECOLÓGICA COSTANERA SUR *Park*

☎ 4893-1588; Av Tristán Achaval Rodríguez 1550, Puerto Madero; 🕑 8am-6pm Tue-Sun Apr-Sep, 8am-7pm Oct-Mar; 🚌 2, 130, 152; 🚶 ♿

Birdwatchers and cyclists find an urban haven in the lovely Reserva Ecológica, a sprawling green space bordered on one side by the Río de la Plata and on the other by the Costanera Sur promenade.

## 🍴 EAT
### 🍴 CABAÑA LAS LILAS
*Parrilla* $$$

☎ 4313-1336; www.laslilas.com, in Spanish; Av Alicia Moreau de Justo 516, Dique 4, Puerto Madero; 🕑 noon-4pm & 7.30pm-1am; Ⓜ Line B LN Alem; ♿ 🚶

Porteños are evenly split as to whether this famous eatery is a fantastically overpriced display of hubris or an upmarket example of *parrilla* perfection. Tellingly, even those who deride this large waterside restaurant won't hesitate to thumb through the jumbo wine list, especially if the meal's on someone else's dime. The fine beef was raised on the restaurant's own *estancia* (ranch).

NEIGHBORHOODS

PUERTO MADERO

### EL MERCADO
*Mediterranean* · $$$
☎ 4010-9200; www.faenahotel
anduniverse.com; Hotel Faena +
Universe, Martha Salotti 445, Dique 2;
⏲ 7am-2am; Ⓜ Line B LN Alem; 🚌 2,
130, 152; ♿

Don't despair if you're not staying at the otherworldly Philippe Starck–designed Faena Hotel + Universe. You can still get a feel for the place at the antique-strewn, shabby chic (emphasis on *chic*) El Mercado, where the stylish set digs into rack of lamb and *empanadas* baked in an adobe mud oven. Award-winning chef Mariano Cid de la Paz presides over the place and El Bistro, its flamboyant sister across the hall – walk by for a glimpse of the blindingly white space with blood-red accents.

### I FRESH MARKET
*Deli, Cafe* $$
☎ 5775-0335; www.ifreshmarket.com.
ar; cnr Azucena Villaflor & Olga Cossettini,
Dique 3, Puerto Madero; ⏲ 8am-late;
🚌 2, 130, 152; ♿ Ⓥ 🚲

This chic deli-cafe-restaurant feels like it belongs in Manhattan, serving espresso and pastries in the morning and fresh vegetable wraps for lunch. The gourmet marketplace inside will tempt you to blow all your cash on rich chocolates and cheeses. For a

Get back to nature at the Reserva Ecológica Costanera Sur (p49)

sophisticated dinner by the water, head to the deli's sister restaurant, i Central Market, on the corner of Dealessi and Güemes.

### 🍴 LA PAROLACCIA DEL MARE
*Italian* $$

☎ 4343-0063; Av Alicia Moreau de Justo 1170, Dique 3, Puerto Madero; ⌚ noon-midnight; Ⓜ Line B LN Alem; Ⓥ

The classy Italian restaurant La Parolaccia has a few locations scattered throughout BA's ritzier barrios; this particular branch specializes in seafood. Reserve a table along the waterfront windows and savor tasty pasta or risotto tossed with freshly caught *mariscos* (shellfish).

## 🍸 DRINK

### 🍸 THE LIBRARY LOUNGE *Bar*

☎ 4010-9200; www.faenahoteland universe.com; Faena Hotel + Universe, Martha Salotti 445, Dique 2, Puerto Madero; ⌚ 9am-2pm; Ⓜ Line B LN Alem; 🚌 2, 130, 152;

The low-lit Library Lounge, all dark wood with plush forest-green armchairs and stuffed moose-heads, feels out of another era. It's the kind of place where gentlemen once gathered to smoke cigars, play billiards and

schmooze. Order a classic martini and let the sultry lounge singer do her thing. Rojo Tango, the sexy cabaret dinner show staged at the adjacent theater, is great, decadent fun – be sure to book ahead.

### 🍸 WHITE BAR *Bar*

☎ 5776-7677; www.hotelmadero.com; Hotel Madero, Rosario Vera Peñaloza 360, Dique 2; ⌚ 7-10:30am, noon-4pm, 7pm-1am; 🚌 2, 130, 152

Lobby bars at five-star hotels often lack character, but the fashionable Hotel Madero, with a long white bar with funky white plastic stools, is an ideal drop-in spot for a pre-dinner cocktail.

## ⭐ PLAY

### 🎭 ASIA DE CUBA *Bar, Club*

☎ 4894-1328; www.asiadecuba.com.ar, in Spanish; Pierina Dealessi 750, Puerto Madero Este; ⌚ 9pm-late Tue-Sat; 🚌 2, 130, 152

This Asian-style lounge bar and club has lost some of its luster in recent years, but the exotic Shanghai-inspired decor and eclectic dance music still bring in well-dressed locals and party-going tourists. The gorgeous cushioned outdoor seating, facing the water, is delightful.

# >CONGRESO & TRIBUNALES

Unlike the various barrios catering to the tourist dollar, Congreso and Tribunales hold fiercely to their stately Spanish roots – the art-nouveau structures along Av de Mayo may be crumbling in places, but they're still there, and traditional cafes still outnumber trendy cocktail bars. This is the 'other' downtown, separated from the Microcentro by Av 9 de Julio. Cross the 16 lanes of speeding traffic to enter this old-fashioned, slightly gritty world where rich and poor often live on the same block. Picturesque Av de Mayo runs through the heart of the barrio and features most of Congreso's historical sites. A compelling range of architectural styles – from enormous belle-epoque edifices around Plaza del Congreso to the neocolonial apartment buildings of Montserrat – make the barrio a fascinating place to wander on a sunny afternoon. The neighborhood is far from being a hot spot for dining and drinking, but traditional Spanish restaurants and cafes proliferate as you walk north through Tribunales toward bustling Av Corrientes, the center of the theater district and home to dozens of pizzerias, cinemas and bookshops. The barrio's crowning glory is the city's grand dame of an opera house, the spectacular Teatro Colón.

## CONGRESO & TRIBUNALES

### 🅞 SEE
El Molino ......................1 B4
Palacio Barolo .............2 C4
Palacio de las Aguas
    Corrientes ..............3 A2
Palacio del Congreso ....4 B4
Plaza del Congreso .......5 C4

### 🅐 SHOP
Arte de Pueblos ...........6 D1
Club de Tango .............7 C3
Gandhi Galerna ...........8 B3

### 🅴 EAT
El Cuartito ...................9 C1
Plaza Asturias ...........10 D4
Restó ........................11 C1
Status .......................12 C4

### 🍸 DRINK
Bar Iberia ..................13 D4
Café Literario Osvaldo
    Bayer ..................14 C4
Cruzat Beer House ......15 C3
El Living ....................16 C1

### ⭐ PLAY
36 Billares .................17 D4
El Beso .....................18 B3
Maluco Beleza ...........19 B3
Teatro Colón ..............20 D2
Teatro Nacional
    Cervantes .............21 D1
Teatro San Martín .......22 C3

# ◉ SEE

## ◉ EL MOLINO

**Av Callao 10, Congreso; Ⓜ Line A Congreso**

This broken-down beauty, reminiscent of Paris' Moulin Rouge, was once an elegant cafe where politicians socialized between meetings at Palacio del Congreso. Sadly, the striking art-nouveau corner building is now covered in cobwebs after closing in 1996. Conservation teams struggle to raise funds to restore El Molino (the Windmill), still considered an architectural landmark.

## ◉ PALACIO BAROLO

**☎ 4383-1065; www.pbarolo.com.ar; Av de Mayo 1370, Congreso; Ⓜ Line A Sáenz Peña, Line B Uruguay**

In 1919, Italian cotton tycoon Luis Barolo commissioned architect Mario Palanti to build a tribute to Dante's *Divine Comedy*. The stunning neo-Gothic Palacio Barolo is the result. It rises 100m and 22 floors – symbolizing the masterpiece's 100 songs, composed of 22 verses each. The floors of the ground level ('Hell') are inlaid with flame-like designs; the next 14 floors, now office space, represent 'Purgatory'; while the uppermost floors and tower, offering spectacular views over the city, are 'Paradise.'

## ◉ PALACIO DE LAS AGUAS CORRIENTES

**☎ 6319-1104; Riobamba 750, Congreso; ◷ 9am-1pm Mon-Fri, closed Jan & Feb; Ⓜ Line D Callao or Facultad de Medicina**

Hundreds of thousands of glazed terracotta tiles adorn the exterior of this awe-inspiring building. Opened in 1894, the fairytale-like Palacio de Las Aguas Corrientes (Palace of Running Water) was home to 12 giant tanks that distributed water to the city. Now the building has a small museum exhibiting antique faucets and urinals.

## ◉ PALACIO DEL CONGRESO

**☎ 4010-3000; cnr Avs Entre Ríos & Rivadavia, Congreso; Ⓜ Line A Congreso; ♿**

The colossal greystone Palacio del Congreso, Argentina's national House of Congress, was structurally inspired by the Capitol in Washington, DC. Completed in 1906, it's topped by an enormous 85m dome and splendid statuary.

## ◉ PLAZA DEL CONGRESO

**Av de Mayo, Congreso; Ⓜ Line A Congreso; ♿**

Plaza del Congreso sees a daily parade of children sprinting toward the carousel, and dog walkers trying to keep up with

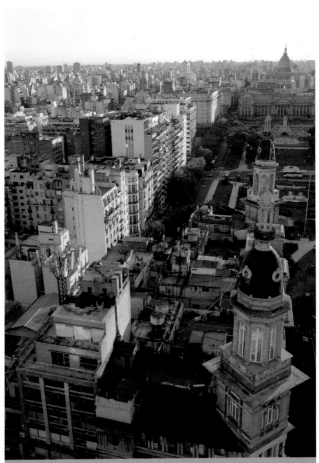

Palacio Barolo watching over Av de Mayo

**GARDEL & THE TANGO**

In June 1935 a woman committed suicide in Havana, and a woman in New York and another in Puerto Rico tried to poison themselves, all over the same man – whom none of them had ever met. This man was tango singer Carlos Gardel, El Zorzal Criollo, the songbird of Buenos Aires, who had just died in a plane crash in Colombia.

Though born in France (or perhaps Uruguay, it's disputed), Gardel was the epitome of the immigrant porteño (BA local). In his youth, he worked at a variety of menial jobs and entertained his neighbors with his rapturous singing. He first performed with Uruguayan-born José Razzano, before collaborating with lyricist Alfredo Le Pera and creating several tango classics such as *Por Una Cabeza*. His beautiful baritone voice, matinee-idol looks and charisma made him a success in Latin America, and later in Paris and New York, during the 1920s and 1930s. His promising career as a Paramount movie star was cut short by the air crash in which his collaborator, Le Pera, was also killed.

A steady procession of pilgrims still visits Carlos Gardel's home (now a museum; see p108) and his sarcophagus in the Cementerio de la Chacarita in Buenos Aires, where a lit cigarette often smolders between the metal fingers of his life-size statue and, as the saying goes, 'Gardel sings better every day.'

their charges. Permanent fixtures include the Monumento a los Dos Congresos, which, with high steps symbolizing the Andes and a fountain representing the Atlantic Ocean, honors the congresses that led Argentina to independence.

## 🛍 SHOP
### 🛍 ARTE DE PUEBLOS
*Souvenirs, Handicrafts*

☎ 4816-4351; www.artedepueblos.org.ar, in Spanish; Libertad 948, Tribunales; 🕑 10am-7:30pm Mon-Fri, 10am-1pm Sat; Ⓜ Line D Tribunales

Shop with a clear conscience at Arte de Pueblos, where fair-trade crafts produced by indigenous

artisans in the Argentine provinces of Salta, Formosa, and Río Negro are available. They use natural materials and traditional techniques to produce this range of wooden utensils, woven belts, ceramic bowls and ethnic jewelry.

### 🛍 CLUB DE TANGO
*Souvenirs*

☎ 4372-7251; www.clubdetango.com.ar, in Spanish; office 114, 5th flr, Paraná 123, Congreso; 🕑 11am-6pm Mon-Fri; Ⓜ Line B Uruguay

Snap up tango souvenirs at this wonderful shop stocked with memorabilia such as Carlos Gardel posters and photo books, and tango lessons on DVD.

## 📖 GANDHI GALERNA
*Bookstore*

☎ 4374-7574; www.galernalibros.com, in Spanish; Av Corrientes 1743, Microcentro; ⏰ 10am-10pm Mon-Thu, 10am- midnight Fri & Sat, 4-10pm Sun; Ⓜ Line B Callao; ♿

If you wear black and keep your mouth shut you might pass for one of the local intellectuals, academics, artists and writers who make this bookshop their second home. Among the philosophy and literature volumes, you'll find tango books and a diverse selection of Latin American music, from *rock nacional* (Argentine rock) to Brazilian samba.

## 🍴 EAT

### 🍽 EL CUARTITO
*Italian, Argentine*                              $

☎ 4816-1758; Talcahuano 937, Tribunales; ⏰ noon-late; Ⓜ Line D Tribunales; 🚌 152, 111; Ⓥ

Since 1934, this legendary pizzeria has seen local men polishing off slices at the counter and families sharing fresh *empanadas* (savory-filled pastries) at tables, surrounded by faded images of sportsmen.

### 🍽 PLAZA ASTURIAS
*Spanish, Seafood*                            $$$

☎ 4382-7334; Cnr Av de Mayo & Salta, Congreso; ⏰ noon-late; Ⓜ Line A Lima; ♿ 🍴

The dated decor at Plaza Asturias assures you that this is no cutting-edge Spanish eatery – no foams, mousses or organic produce here, just heaping portions of shrimp, mussels and clams tossed with garlic and herbs. Try the pungent *cazuela de mariscos* (seafood stew; a flavorful antidote to the meat-heavy cuisine at other restaurants) that will jolt your palate and clear up your sinuses.

### 🍽 RESTÓ
*Modern Argentine, French*          $$

☎ 4816-6711; Montevideo 938, Tribunales; ⏰ 8:30-11pm Thu & Fri; Ⓜ Line D Callao

María Barrutia's painstakingly artistic presentations of quail and salmon contrast sharply with her restaurant's understated environs. The illustrious chef whips up slow food that is either a smash hit – a rich, creamy pumpkin soup – or a flop. Either way, she's experimental, and she makes a splash on the local dining scene. Try her creative daily menu at Restó.

### 🍽 STATUS *Peruvian*                      $

☎ 4382-8531; Virrey Cevallos 178, Congreso; ⏰ noon-5pm & 8pm-1am Mon-Thu, noon-1am Fri-Sun; Ⓜ Line A Sáenz Peña; Ⓥ ♿

Raw shark and a purple corn cocktail? It tastes much better than it sounds, Status' devotees will guarantee you. This no-frills eatery, packing in a nightly crowd with roasted chicken and rice, fresh shark *ceviche* (lemon-marinated fish), creamy potatoes and cinnamon-topped pisco sours, is a gastronomic standout in a part of town that's rife with traditional Peruvian restaurants.

# DRINK

## BAR IBERIA *Cafe, Bar*

☎ 4381-6300; cnr Av de Mayo & Salta, Congreso; ☼ 24hr; Ⓜ Line A Lima; 🚻 ♿

Soak up the grandeur of Av de Mayo at Bar Iberia, the city's second-oldest cafe. Since 1897, the sophisticated corner bar has welcomed distinguished clientele like playwright Federico García Lorca, who lived for a time at the nearby Castelar Hotel. Take in the avenue's magnificent architecture from the sidewalk table.

## CAFÉ LITERARIO OSVALDO BAYER *Cafe*

☎ 4382-3261; Hipólito Yrigoyen 1584, Congreso; ☼ 8:30am-10:30pm Mon-Fri, 11am-5pm Sat; Ⓜ Line A Congreso, Line A Sáenz Peña

The Madres de la Plaza de Mayo run this small cafe and eatery, in conjunction with the bookstore at their headquarters – a hub of liberal politics where students scan the papers to see if any children of the *desaparecidos* (disappeared ones) have been located. The cafe is modest, but the atmosphere is unique. See also p17.

## CRUZAT BEER HOUSE *Bar*

☎ 6320-5344; www.cruzatba.com; Sarmiento 1617, Congreso; ☼ 10am-2am Mon-Thu, to 4am Fri & Sat; Ⓜ Line B Callao

---

### WORTH THE TRIP

Located way out in the western suburbs, the lighthearted folk festival **Feria de Mataderos** ( ☎ 4687-5602; www.feriademataderos.com.ar, in Spanish; cnr Avs Lisandro de la Torre & de los Corrales; ☼ 1-9pm Sun & holidays Apr-Nov, 6pm-midnight Sat Dec-Mar) will take almost an hour to reach by bus 155 or 126 – but the journey's worth it. Brilliantly costumed teenagers perform folkloric dances on stage while gauchos on horseback compete in traditional contests and local ladies dish out hearty country-style food and sweet *patero* wine. Over 100 craft stalls sell affordable handmade treasures from horse-hoof ashtrays to leather and metalwork; indulge yourself along the strip of gourmet food stalls where vendors offer free samples of *dulce de leche* liqueur, cheeses, and homemade liquors. For details on upcoming festivals, check their website. The long bus ride to Mataderos is a cultural experience in itself – but travelers on a strict schedule can also arrive by taxi.

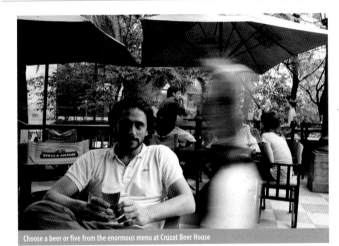

Choose a beer or five from the enormous menu at Cruzat Beer House

In wine-soaked Buenos Aires, Cruzat is as close as you can get to a German beer garden. Kick back on the shaded terrace and choose from a thick menu of over 150 microbrews – or ask for the beer tasting. A selection of a dozen draught beers, served in miniature glasses, will come right to your table.

### ☎ EL LIVING Bar, Club
☎ 4811-4730; www.living.com.ar, in Spanish; Marcelo T de Alvear 1540, Retiro; ☼ 7pm-3am Thu, 10pm-6am Fri & Sat; 🚌 10, 39, 102, 152

Laid-back El Living (the Living Room) sticks to a decade-old formula: plush sofas, cheap whiskey sours, campy George Michael music videos projected onto a huge screen, and a young, cheerful crowd. Before 2am, dinner guests linger and most bar stools are empty, but you'll be squished between vintage Madonna fans when the '80s dance party gets going in the wee hours.

## ⭐ PLAY

### ⭐ 36 BILLARES Billiards, Tango
☎ 4381-5696; www.los36billares.com.ar; Av de Mayo 1265, Congreso; ☼ 8am-2am; Ⓜ Line A Lima

Shoot pool with some elderly gents – or just catch a performance by a sultry singer in the main cafe –

at this antique bar where the Argentine Billiards Association was born in 1926. The nightly tango show verges on the burlesque.

### ⭐ EL BESO Tango
☎ 4953-2794; Riobamba 416, Tribunales; ⌚ from 10:30pm Wed, 6pm Thu, 10:30pm Fri & Sat, 10pm Sun; Ⓜ Line B Callao

This traditional tango salon brings in some 2000 *tangueros* (traditional tango dancers) every week for its dynamic *milongas* (social dances) and daily classes. Despite the increased presence of curious tourists, El Beso maintains a wonderfully authentic atmosphere.

### ⭐ MALUCO BELEZA
Dance Club
☎ 4372-1737; www.malucobeleza .com.ar, in Spanish; Sarmiento 1728, Tribunales; ⌚ 1am-late Wed & Fri-Sun; Ⓜ Line B Callao

This energetic Brazilian club is the place to go when you're experiencing tango overload. If samba's not your thing, there's house music upstairs.

### ⭐ TEATRO COLÓN Theater
☎ 4378-7344; Libertad 621, Tribunales, tours depart from Tucumán 1171; ⌚ performance times vary; Ⓜ Line D Tribunales; 🚌 23, 29, 39, 75, 99, 102, 115, 140; ♿ ♿

After painstakingly time-consuming renovations, the fabulous Teatro Colón – dating from 1908 and considered one of the world's great opera houses – finally reopened its doors to the public in May 2010. Sink into a red velvet seat to enjoy a classical concert, opera or theatre production in this renowned performance space that ballet dancer Mikhail Baryshnikov called 'the most beautiful of the theaters I know.'

## CONTEMPORARY GALLERIES

Intrigued by Buenos Aires' edgy art scene? Stop by one of the major galleries to behold creative works from photography to sculpture – or, better yet, show up at an exhibition opening to sip champagne and check out the art folk in action. On the north side of the city, **Braga Menendez Arte Contemporaneo** (Map pp114-15, C3; ☎ 4775-5577; www .galeriabm.com; Humboldt 1574, Villa Crespo; ⌚ 1-8pm Mon-Fri & 2-6pm Sat-Sun; closed Jan-Feb) shows contemporary work by dozens of independent artists. Downtown, swing by a tried-and-true art institution, **Ruth Benzacar** (Map p63, C3; ☎ 4313-8480; www .ruthbenzacar.com; Florida 1000, Retiro; ⌚ 11:30am-8pm Mon-Fri), or continue south to San Telmo's stylish new **Zavaleta Lab** (Map p71, B2; ☎ 4342-9293; www.zavaletalab.com; Venezuela 567, San Telmo; ⌚ 11am-8pm Mon-Fri & 11am-2pm Sat).

## WORTH THE TRIP

The venue is off the beaten path, but true tango enthusiasts shouldn't forgo a trip to El Niño Bien, one of the city's most atmospheric *milongas*. Held on Thursday nights at the **Centro Region Leonesa** ( ☎ 4147-8867; Humberto Primo 1462; admission $20; ☷ 6pm-late Mon & Fri, 11pm-late Thu, from 4pm Sat & Sun; g39, 60, 102), the event sees porteño couples embracing and twirling dramatically around a spectacular wooden dance floor as strains of Carlos Gardel's 'Mi Noche Triste' (My Sad Night) crackle through the antique sound system. El Niño Bien is charmingly local – in other words, not designed for tourists – so if you're just going to observe the scene, don't blind the dancers with your camera flash. Just grab a table for two and play it cool with a bottle of Cabernet. Consider booking ahead, as the regular *tangueros* are quick to snap up the tables skirting the dance floor. If you're not in town on a Thursday, catch the afternoon *milonga* here on Wednesdays and Fridays, or swing by after dinner – the building hosts low-key *milongas* most nights of the week.

### ✪ TEATRO NACIONAL CERVANTES *Theater*

☎ 4816-4224; www.teatrocervantes
.gov.ar, in Spanish; Libertad 815, Tribunales; ☷ box office 10am-8pm, closed
Jan; Ⓜ Line D Tribunales; ♿ ♿
This architectural gem, featuring an ornate lobby and sumptuous velvet seats, is a classic venue to catch musicals and dance performances.

### ✪ TEATRO SAN MARTÍN *Theater*

☎ 0800-333-5254; www.teatrosanmar
tin.com.ar; Av Corrientes 1530, Tribunales;
☷ performance times vary; Ⓜ Line B
Uruguay; ▣ 24, 60, 102; ♿ ♿
This 1970s-style theater may lack old-fashioned charm, but the diverse agenda of Spanish ballet, children's musicals, French plays, classic films and alternative theater makes San Martín a staple of the Corrientes strip.

# >RETIRO

In Spanish, Retiro means 'retreat,' which refers to the country villa and surrounding gardens that Spanish politician Agustín de Robles established here in the late 17th century. Lovely Plaza San Martín, with its twisting *palo rosa* trees and sloping green lawn, still conjures up images of the original estate – but yesterday's aristocracy would be shocked to see that today's Retiro also contains one of the city's largest *villas* (shantytowns). Apart from the poverty-stricken encampment that sprawls northward from the central train station, the barrio is stylish and upscale, boasting several ritzy hotels and palaces, architectural landmarks like the Edificio Kavanagh and the Torre de los Ingleses, and a number of fashionable bistros and bars that line San Martín and its parallel street Reconquista. Fans of writer Jorge Luis Borges can take a look at his modest apartment building at Maipú 994.

## RETIRO

### ● SEE
Edificio Kavanagh .......... **1** D3
Museo Municipal de Arte
   Hispanoamericano Isaac
   Fernández Blanco .......**2** B2
Plaza San Martín ..........**3** C3
Torre de los Ingleses ......**4** D2

### ⬛ SHOP
Autoría ..........................**5** B3
Casa Lopez ....................**6** C3

El Remanso ...................**7** C3
JCB Gems & Carvings .....**8** C3
Ligier ...........................**9** C3
Tierra Adentro ............**10** B2

### 🍴 EAT
El Establo ....................**11** D3
El Federal ....................**12** D3
Empire Thai .................**13** D4
Filo .............................**14** D3
Le Sud ........................**15** C2
Sipan ..........................**16** C4

### ▼ DRINK
Café Retiro ..................**17** C2
Dadá ...........................**18** D3
Marriott Plaza Bar .......**19** C3

### ★ PLAY
ND/Ateneo ..................**20** B4

Río
de la
Plata

Reserva
Ecológica
Costanera
Sur

Av Tristán Achával Rodríguez

See Puerto Madero
Map p47

200 m
0.1 miles

Dársena
Norte

Puerto
Madero

Dique
No 4

Av Commodore Py

Av Alicia Moreau de Justo

Av Antártida Argentina

Bouchard

Av E de Basti

Av Eduardo Madero

Manuel Tienda León
Downtown Office

25 de Mayo

Av Leandro N Alem

Tucumán

Retiro Bus
Terminal

Av Ramos Mejía

Plaza
Canadá

Torre Bank
Boston

Torre
IBM

Torre Catalinas
Plaza

Torre
Alem Plaza

Laminar Plaza

Reconquista

Av Eduardo Madero

Plaza
Zuviría
del Carril

San Martín

Dr Rojas

Tres Sargentos

San Martín

Retiro

4

Plaza Fuerza
Aérea Argentina

12

14

18

Florida

Viamonte

See Microcentro
Map p37

Estación
Retiro

17

Retiro

3

Plaza San
Martín

Marcelo T de Alvear

1

Ruth
Benzacar

19

Microcentro

Basavilbaso

Palacio
San Martín

Av Santa Fe

6

8

16

Maipú

Esmeralda

San
Martín

Retiro Bus
Tourist Kiosk

Borges
apartment

7

9

Paraguay

Av Córdoba

Esmeralda

15

10

2

Esmeralda

Secretaría
de Turismo
de la Nación

5

9

Av Santa Fe

Suipacha

Suipacha

Quiroga

Arroyo

Carlos Pellegrini

20

Av 9 de Julio

Av 9 de Julio

Carlos Pellegrini

Cerrito

Cerrito

Plaza
Libertad

See Recoleta & Barrio Norte
Map p91

Av del Libertador

Patio
Bullrich

Libertad

Av Pellegrini

Parera

Av Quintana

Libertad

Av Santa Fe

Juncal

Arenales

Marcelo T de Alvear

Paraguay

Av Córdoba

Talcahuano

Plaza
Lavalle

See Congreso & Tribunales
Map p53

Posadas

Av Alvear

Recoleta

Uruguay

# 👁 SEE

## 👁 EDIFICIO KAVANAGH

**Florida 1035, Retiro;** Ⓜ **Line C San Martín**
A feisty Irishwoman funded
the construction of this handsome 120m art-deco apartment
building, which was the tallest
skyscraper in Latin America at the
time of its construction in 1935.
A local rumor claims that the
heiress, vengeful towards another
aristocratic family for scorning her
daughter, built the structure that
high to block light from entering
the basilica where her rivals attended Mass every Sunday.

## 👁 MUSEO MUNICIPAL DE ARTE HISPANOAMERICANO ISAAC FERNÁNDEZ BLANCO

☎ **4327-0228; Suipacha 1422; admission
$3, free on Thu;** 🕑 **2-7pm Tue-Sun;**
🚌 **93, 130, 152**
Situated in a Peruvian-inspired
baroque mansion, this museum
displays Latin American colonial art including Jesuit statuary,
engravings, textiles, silver and
antiques. Chamber orchestra
performances enliven the lovely
Spanish-style gardens during
the warmer months (October to
April).

## 👁 PLAZA SAN MARTÍN

**Av Santa Fe & Florida, Retiro;** Ⓜ **Line C
San Martín;** ♿

Carlos Thays designed Plaza San
Martín, the center's prettiest green
space, on a gently sloping bluff.
The park benches fill quickly on
warm afternoons with sandwich-
toting accountants and amorous
couples. The imposing bronze
and marble monument honors
the South American liberator San
Martín.

## 👁 TORRE DE LOS INGLESES

**Plaza Fuerza Aérea Argentina, Retiro;**
Ⓜ **Line C San Martín**
Big Ben in Buenos Aires. This
76m clock tower, located just
across Plaza San Martín (left),
was donated by the city's British
community in 1910. Decades later,
it was a bomb target during the
1982 Falklands War.

# 🛍 SHOP

## 🛍 AUTORÍA

*Art, Home Decor*
☎ **5252-2474; www.autoriabsas
.com.ar, in Spanish; Suipacha 1025,
Retiro;** 🕑 **9:30am-8pm Mon-Fri,
10am-2pm & 4:30-8pm Sat;** Ⓜ **Line C
San Martín**
This cool designers' showcase,
stocked with make-a-statement
silver jewelry, edgy art books and
whimsical leather desk sculptures,
brings a welcome taste of the
avant-garde to this suit-and-tie
neighborhood.

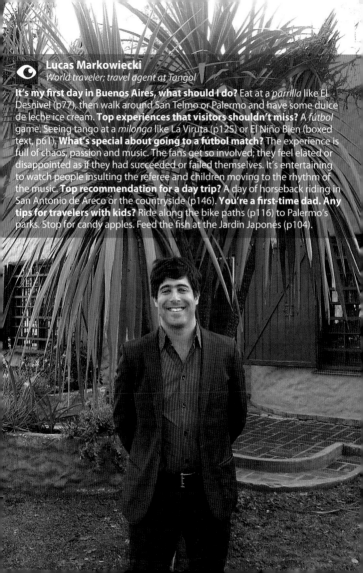

**Lucas Markowiecki**
*World traveler; travel agent at Tangol*

**It's my first day in Buenos Aires, what should I do?** Eat at a *parrilla* like El Desnivel (p77), then walk around San Telmo or Palermo and have some dulce de leche ice cream. **Top experiences that visitors shouldn't miss?** A *fútbol* game. Seeing tango at a *milonga* like La Viruta (p125) or El Niño Bien (boxed text, p61). **What's special about going to a fútbol match?** The experience is full of chaos, passion and music. The fans get so involved; they feel elated or disappointed as if they had succeeded or failed themselves. It's entertaining to watch people insulting the referee and children moving to the rhythm of the music. **Top recommendation for a day trip?** A day of horseback riding in San Antonio de Areco or the countryside (p146). **You're a first-time dad. Any tips for travelers with kids?** Ride along the bike paths (p116) to Palermo's parks. Stop for candy apples. Feed the fish at the Jardín Japonés (p104).

NEIGHBORHOODS

RETIRO

### 🏠 CASA LOPEZ *Leather*
☎ 4311-3044; www.casalopez.com
.ar; Marcelo T de Alvear 640/658, Retiro;
🕐 9am-8pm Mon-Fri, 10am-6:30pm Sat
& Sun; Ⓜ Line C San Martín

For boots and briefcases that'll last
a lifetime, head to Casa Lopez, a
shop that's been selling high-
quality leather jackets, luggage,
bags and accessories since 1943.
Go elsewhere for youthful fashion –
the style here is conservative and
classic.

### 🏠 EL REMANSO *Leather*
☎ 4312-1879; Esmeralda 1018, Retiro;
🕐 9am-7pm Mon-Fri, 10am-5pm Sat;
Ⓜ Line C San Martín

The city's suavest gentlemen –
polo players, obviously – roll
up to outfitters like this one for
dapper leather boots and stylish
riding gear fit for their chiseled
physiques. See the thoroughbreds
in action at the polo grounds in
Las Cañitas (p133).

### 🏠 JCB GEMS & CARVINGS
*Jewelry, Souvenirs*
☎ 4312-7517; Paraguay 627; 🕐 10am-
8pm Mon-Fri, 10am-6pm Sat; Ⓜ Line C
San Martín

Woo your sweetheart (or treat
yourself) with the romantic
petal-pink *rodocrosita*, Argentina's unofficial national stone.
This family-run gem and mineral
shop carries artisan-produced

pieces from gemstone earrings to
handcrafted silver bracelets.

### 🏠 LIGIER *Wine, Gourmet Deli*
☎ 4515-0126; www.ligier.com.ar, in
Spanish; cnr Av Santa Fe & Esmeralda, Retiro; 🕐 9:30am-8pm Mon-Fri, 10am-2pm
& 4-8pm Sat; Ⓜ Line C San Martín; ♿

This upmarket *vinoteca* and
gourmet food chain deals primarily with tourists, which explains
cheesy packages like the Teatro
Colón wine collection. Nonethe-
less, Ligier is a foolproof stop
when you need to pick up last-
minute gifts (or a bottle of bubbly
to take back to the hotel room).

### 🏠 TIERRA ADENTRO
*Souvenirs, Handicrafts*
☎ 4393-8552; Arroyo 882,
Retiro; 🕐 10am-8pm Mon-Fri, 10am-
6pm Sat; 🚌 93, 130, 152

Tierra Adentro works with
nonprofit organizations to help
preserve indigenous communities
in northern Argentina. Fair-trade
practices brought this fine range
of hand-woven cushion covers,
colorful wall hangings and striking
Mapuche silver necklaces to the
capital city.

## 🍴 EAT

### 🍴 EL ESTABLO *Parrilla*                $$
☎ 4311-1639; Paraguay 489, Retiro;
🕐 7am-2am; Ⓜ Line C San Martín; ♿ 🚻

While it gets its fair share of tourists, El Establo is unlikely to have a tango show or wi-fi anytime soon. Try the Spanish tapas paired with the house red, then turn your attention to the true star of the show, the skillful *parrillero* (grill man).

### 🍴 EL FEDERAL *Argentine* $$
☎ 4313-1324; San Martin 1015, Retiro; ⏱ 10am-midnight Mon-Fri, to 6pm Sat; Ⓜ Line C San Martín

This traditional corner eatery serves Argentinian comfort food – simple pastas, steaks and *empanadas* – as well as higher-end specialties like Patagonian lamb. The old-school waiters and rustic wooden bar add charm.

### 🍴 EMPIRE THAI *Thai* $$$
☎ 4312-5706; www.empirethai.net; Tres Sargentos 427, Retiro; ⏱ noon-1am Mon-Fri, 7pm-2am Sat; 🚌 93, 152; ♿ Ⓥ

The sultry lighting and sumptuous decor are your first clue that this place isn't a traditional ethnic diner; the second is when you're still hungry after finishing your noodles. Never mind – the scrumptious peanut satay and the moody New York ambiance draw a cool crowd, and flavors like coconut and lemongrass give your palate a rest from all the steak you've probably consumed elsewhere.

### 🍴 FILO *Italian* $$
☎ 4311-0312; www.filo-ristorante.com, in Spanish; San Martín 975, Retiro; ⏱ noon-midnight; Ⓜ Line C San Martin; ♿ Ⓥ 🍽

Popular with the 45-minutes-and-gone business lunch crowd and, by night, couples out on their third dinner date, this large, pop-art-style Italian pizzeria tosses thin-crust pies with fresh toppings.

Pizza and art are side by side at Filo restaurant

Try one piled high with prosciutto and arugula, then throw back some limoncello before checking out the downstairs art gallery.

### 🍴 LE SUD
*French*                                    $$$

☎ 4131-0130; Sofitel, Arroyo 841, Retiro; 🕒 6:30-11am, 12:30-3pm, & 7:30pm-midnight; 🚌 93, 130, 152; 👤 V

At the Hotel Sofitel's buttoned-up French eatery, Chef Olivier Falchi whips out simple yet authentic fusion cuisine sprinkled with fresh herbs, spices and oils from the Mediterranean. Chandeliers and marble add formality that's absent from the casual downtown brasseries.

### 🍴 SIPAN *Peruvian, Japanese* $$$

☎ 4315-0763; www.sipan.com.ar, in Spanish; Paraguay 624, Microcentro; 🕒 noon-4pm & 8pm-1am Mon-Sat; Ⓜ Line C San Martín

Japanese-Peruvian food is all the rage in Buenos Aires. Skip the pretentious Palermo eateries peddling overpriced ceviche and taste-test the fresh, flavorful cuisine at Sipan. Tucked away in an unsuspecting shopping gallery, this low-lit pisco bar turns out imaginative seafood tapas, served heaping on ceramic spoons, and mouthwatering cocktails made with pisco the owners smuggled over from Peru.

## 🍸 DRINK

### 🍸 CAFÉ RETIRO *Cafe*

☎ 4516-0902; Estación Retiro (Retiro Station Lobby), Ramos Meija 1358, Retiro; 🕒 6:30am-10pm; Ⓜ Line C Retiro; 👤 ♿

Catching a train out of town? Allow an extra half-hour for coffee at this grand cafe in the main hall – the soaring ceilings, polished wood and bronze interior and bustling train station will make you feel like the star of a silent movie.

### JORGE LUIS BORGES

Jorge Luis Borges (1899–1986) is Argentina's controversial literary hero. A linguist, poet and professor, Borges adored English literature – and though his countrymen chided him for being Anglocentric, he put his passion to practice and became a highly respected translator of Walt Whitman's poetry. Despite criticism from porteños and the cold shoulder from the Nobel Prize committee, Borges enjoyed popularity and acclaim abroad upon the publication of his short story collection *Labyrinths*, and literary scholars say that his handling of mythology and realism influenced many writers in Latin America, including Gabriel García Márquez. If you're near Plaza San Martín (p64), stroll past Maipú 994 and look up at the modest 6th-floor apartment where the literary legend lived and worked for a time.

Order a classic drink at the Marriott Plaza Bar

 **DADÁ** *Bar, Restaurant*
☎ 4314-4787; San Martín 941, Retiro;
🕑 noon-2am Mon-Sat; Ⓜ Line C San
Martín
The tiny bohemian Dadá, cluttered
with wine bottles and with walls
painted red, feels like an unassum-
ing neighborhood bar in Paris. Get
cozy with a varietal from a boutique bodega and order something
savory off the bistro menu – the
fresh guacamole and homemade
potato chips are perfect for
sharing – in this room full of
easygoing waiters, intellectuals and
groups of laughing friends.

 **MARRIOTT PLAZA BAR** *Bar*
☎ 4318-3000; Basement, Marriott Plaza
Hotel, Florida 1005, Retiro; 🕑 11am-
1am; Ⓜ Line C San Martín; ♿
Yeah, yeah – drinks at the Marriott
doesn't sound like a winning cul-

tural experience. But this palatial
century-old hotel wasn't always
part of the mainstream chain. Designed by Alfred Zucker, the man
responsible for St Patrick's Cathedral in New York, it still boasts a
genteel art-deco bar with cordial
service and classic cocktails.

## ★ PLAY

★ **ND/ATENEO** *Concert Venue*
☎ 4328-2888; www.ndateneo.com.ar,
in Spanish; Paraguay 918, Retiro; 🕑 box
office noon-8pm Mon-Sat; 🚌 10, 21, 39,
102, 152; ♿
This gorgeous restored theater
dates back to the 1930s. Best-
known for hosting the Buenos
Aires International Jazz Festival,
the venue sees performances by
tango legends and folk musicians
on weekends. Get tickets from the
box office or www.plateanet.com.

# >SAN TELMO

Colorful San Telmo is a neighborhood in flux. Once an elegant colonial quarter of Spanish aristocrats, the barrio fell into near-ruin after the yellow fever epidemic of 1871 pushed the beau monde to higher ground and poor Italian immigrants turned the once-grand mansions into tenement housing. Porteños (BA locals) have long considered San Telmo – and its cobbled streets lined with dilapidated art-nouveau buildings, traditional *parrillas* (grill restaurants) and faded old cafes – to be run-down and dangerous. But thanks to sentimental locals and foreigners thrilled by the old-world atmosphere, money is pouring into the neighborhood. Even as sagging balconies are replaced, much of San Telmo's broken-down charm is alive and well in its crumbling facades and bohemian population. By day its narrow streets clamor with construction workers tripping across decaying sidewalks and tourists trolling the row of antique shops; at night, tango clubs fill with patrons and Plaza Dorrego throngs with a lighthearted crowd hanging around for cold *cerveza* (beer) and live music.

## SAN TELMO

### 🅒 SEE
El Zanjón de Granados ...1　C3
Museo Histórico
　　Nacional ....................2　C5
Parque Lezama ..............3　C5
Plaza Dorrego ...............4　C4

### 🅒 SHOP
Artesanos de Argentina ..5　C4
El Buen Orden ...............6　C4
Feria San Pedro Telmo ..(see 4)
Gabriel del Campo
　　Anticuario .................7　C3
Gil Antigüedades ...........8　C4
HB Antiques ...................9　C4
Imhotep ......................10　C3
L'Ago .........................11　C3
L'Ago .........................12　C3
Materia Urbana ............13　C3
Mercado de San Telmo ..14　B3
Moebius .....................15　C5

Pablo Ramírez .............16　B2
Puntos en el Espacio ....17　B3
Ruffino Bazar & Vinos ..18　B3
Walrus Books ..............19　B3

### 🍴 EAT
Amici Miei ...................20　C4
Brasserie Petanque ......21　C2
Café San Juan .............22　C4
Comedor Nikkai ...........23　B3
El Desnivel ..................24　C3
Gran Parrilla del Plata ..25　B3
La Vinería de
　　Gualterio Bolívar ......26　B3
Manolo .......................27　B4
Matilda's Café .............28　B3
Origen .......................29　B4
Parrilla 1880 ...............30　C5
Sagardi Euskal
　　Taberna ...................31　C4
Taberna Baska .............32　A3

### 🍸 DRINK
647 ............................33　A3
Bar Británico ...............34　C5
Bar Plaza Dorrego ....(see 4)
Bar Seddón .................35　C3
Doppelgänger .............36　B5
El Federal ...................37　B3
Gibraltar ....................38　B3
La Puerta Roja ............39　B3
Pride Café ..................40　C3

### ⭐ PLAY
Bar Sur ......................41　C3
Centro Cultural
　　Torquato Tasso ........42　C5
El Querandí .................43　B2
El Viejo Almacén .........44　C3
La Cumparsita .............45　B3
La Trastienda ..............46　C2
Museum .....................47　B2

# SEE

## EL ZANJÓN DE GRANADOS

☎ 4361-3002; www.elzanjon.com.
ar; Defensa 755, San Telmo; admission/
tour $36, shorter tour on Sun for $18;
🕑 11am-4pm Mon-Fri, 1-6pm Sun;
🚌 10, 20, 22, 29, 86; ♿
Peek into the city's past at El Zanjón, an exquisitely restored urban
villa and archeological site. Once
the private residence of wealthy
Spanish settlers, the abandoned
mansion later became communal
living space for immigrant families.
In 1985, a local historian purchased
the property and discovered a
reservoir of antique treasures
among the rubble in a series of
underground tunnels. Today's
tour guides lead visitors past the
open-air water cistern and through
the subterranean labyrinth, point-
ing out displays of French tiles,
children's toys and other remnants
of daily life in gentler times.

## MUSEO HISTÓRICO NACIONAL

☎ 4307-1182; cnr Defensa & Av Caseros,
San Telmo; admission $4; 🕑 11am-6pm
Wed-Sun, closed Jan; 🚌 29, 39, 53, 64
Housed in an old mansion on the
edge of leafy Parque Lezama (right),
this small museum offers an over-
view of Argentina's history. Displays
of antique furniture, weaponry,
clothing and artwork illustrate the

nation's progress from the pre-
Columbian era to independence.

## PARQUE LEZAMA

Defensa & Av Brasil, San Telmo; 🚌 10,
22, 29, 39; ♿
Scruffy Parque Lezama was once
thought to be the site of Buenos
Aires' founding in 1536, but archeological teams recently refuted
the hypothesis. Today's green park
hosts old chess-playing gentlemen,
bookworms toting mate (traditional Argentine tea) gourds and
teenagers kissing on park benches.
Don't miss the striking Iglesia
Ortodoxa Rusa (Russian Orthodox
Church) on the north side of the
park.

### FILETE PORTEÑO

It's said that while tango is an expression of sadness, filete – Buenos Aires'
other folk art – is a celebration. Walk
around San Telmo and you'll see the
finely painted linework, curlicues and
flowers of filete, a decorative painting
style that emerged at the end of the
19th century as a form of distinguishing
horse-drawn carts. The style moved to
trucks and later to public buses, until the
military government of 1976–83 out-
lawed filete on public transport. Today,
several fileteadores (painters) sell works
to tourists at craft markets and offer
beginner-level filete lessons; you'll see
their public work throughout San Telmo,
Congreso and La Boca.

## ☉ PLAZA DORREGO

**Defensa & Humberto Primo, San Telmo;**
🚌 **10, 22, 29, 45, 86;** ♿

This vibrant colonial square, one of the city's oldest, is a hub of activity. Guitar-strumming artisans line the plaza with displays of silver jewelry and leather belts while cafe-dwellers kick back at plastic tables for conversation and tango performances. Pull up a chair, order a pitcher of sangria-like *clericot de vino,* and ward off the parade of magazine vendors with a polite but firm 'no gracias' (no, thank you).

# 🛍 SHOP

## ☐ ARTESANOS DE ARGENTINA
*Souvenirs, Handicrafts*

☎ **4300-5791; www.artesanosdesan telmo.com.ar, in Spanish; Defensa 1281, San Telmo;** ☽ **10am-7pm;** 🚌 **10, 22, 29**

Support local artisans (and save a few pesos) at this wonderful co-op full of wooden dishes, hand-painted leather sandals, natural cigars, *dulce de leche* liqueur and *mate* gourds. The craftsmen are friendly and eager to please at this large store straddling Defensa.

## ☐ EL BUEN ORDEN
*Antiques, Fashion*

☎ **4307-8608; www.elbuenorden.com. ar; Defensa 894, San Telmo;** ☽ **11am-7pm;** 🚌 **10, 22, 29, 45, 86**

Dig for vintage treasures in this jam-packed little shop. If you have the patience to sort through shelves full of costume jewelry, Jackie O–style sunglasses, old lace, opera gloves, assorted figurines and old-fashioned ice skates, you might come away with the perfect pillbox hat or pearl brooch.

## ☐ FERIA SAN PEDRO TELMO
*Market*

**Defensa, San Telmo;** ☽ **10am-6pm Sun;** 🚌 **10, 22, 29, 45, 86**

On Sundays, San Telmo's main drag is closed to traffic and the street is a sea of local families and tourists browsing craft stalls, waiting at vendor's carts for freshly squeezed orange juice, poking through the antique glass ornaments on display on Plaza Dorrego (left), and listening to street performances by tango orchestras.

## ☐ GIL ANTIGÜEDADES
*Antiques, Fashion*

☎ **4361-5019; www.gilantiguedades .com.ar; Humberto Primo 412, San Telmo;** ☽ **11am-1pm & 3-7pm Tue-Sat, 11am-7pm Sun;** 🚌 **10, 22, 29, 45, 86**

A window display of Great Gatsby–style flapper dresses and vintage nightgowns pulls passersby into San Telmo's finest antiques emporium. Decorative objects like china teapots and leather hatboxes are overshadowed by the stunning array of silk slips and lacy Victorian gowns – Famous names like John Galliano, Catherine Deneuve and Salvatore Ferragamo have shopped here.

### 📷 L'AGO Home Decor, Souvenirs

☎ 4362-3641; www.lagosantelmo.com; Defensa 919 & 970, San Telmo; ⏱ 10am-7:30pm; 🚌 10, 22, 29, 45, 86

Kitschy-cool home decor, from fluorescent-hued *mate* sets to Frida Kahlo kitchen magnets, attracts hipsters and travelers to cute-as-a-button L'Ago. They have two stores located across the street from each other; don't miss buttery handmade soaps scented like chocolate, coffee and passion fruit.

### 📷 MATERIA URBANA
Design, Home Decor

☎ 4361-5265; www.materiaurbana .com, in Spanish; Defensa 707, San Telmo;

⏱ 10am-7pm Mon-Sat, 10am-8pm Sun; 🚌 10, 22, 29, 39, 86

This innovative design shop shows the work of over 100 local artists; one-of-a-kind finds include offbeat line drawings, abstract photography and jewelry made from silver, wood and coral. There's nearly constant traffic at Materia Urbana, especially during the street fair on Sundays; for a calmer shopping experience, stop by on a weekday.

### 🏛 MERCADO DE SAN TELMO
Market, Antiques

Defensa, Bolívar, Carlos Calvo & Estados Unidos block, San Telmo; ⏱ 10am-7pm; 🚌 10, 22, 29, 39, 86

Occupying an entire city block, this market was built in 1897 by Juan Antonio Buschiazzo, the same Italian-born Argentine architect who designed the Recoleta Cemetery (p93.) The wrought-iron interior and glass skylights make it one of BA's most atmospheric

---

## A CABINET OF CURIOSITIES

San Telmo is famous for its myriad shops crammed with antiques, curios and collectibles. Poke around in these locales to find old-fashioned treasures from vintage suitcases to ivory busts and Bakelite bangles.

> **Gabriel del Campo Anticuario** ( ☎ 4361-2061; Defensa 990; ⏱ 10am-7pm) Eclectic objects from antique tin toys to retro luggage.

> **HB Antiques** ( ☎ 4361-3325; www.hbantiques.com.ar; Defensa 1016; ⏱ 10am-7pm Mon-Fri, 11am-5pm Sun) Classy art-deco antiques and paintings in a grand showroom.

> **Imhotep** ( ☎ 4862-9298; Defensa 916; ⏱ 11am-6pm Sun-Fri) An offbeat collection of Chinese snuff boxes, mini gargoyles, religious figurines, knickknacks and home decor.

Moebius boutique is waiting to dress you

markets; it's also where locals shop for fresh produce, cheese and meat. Look for secondhand leather luggage, delicate wine decanters and Jackie O–style sunglasses at the peripheral antique stalls.

### MOEBIUS *Women's Fashion*
☎ 4361-2893; Defensa 1356, San Telmo; 🕙 10am-1pm & 3-8:30pm Tue-Sat, 11am-8:30pm Sun; 🚌 10, 22, 24, 29, 39
This funky little shop feels like the walk-in closet of the fashionable artist sister you never had: the racks are crowded with owner-designer Lilliana Zauberman's kaleidoscopic 1970s-style jersey dresses, whimsical ruffled bikinis, skirts printed with koi fish and frog patterns, cherry-red trench coats and handbags made from recycled materials.

### PABLO RAMÍREZ *Fashion*
☎ 4342-7154; www.pabloramirez.com.ar; Perú 587, San Telmo; 🕙 10:30am-7:30pm Mon-Fri, 10:30am-3pm Sat; Ⓜ Line E Belgrano
Stark black, crisp white and pared-down sophistication characterize the men's and women's collections by this venerated porteño designer. A must-see for fashionistas who've strayed south from the Palermo boutique circuit.

### PUNTOS EN EL ESPACIO *Fashion, Shoes*
☎ 4307-1742; www.puntosenelespacio.com.ar; Perú 979, San Telmo; 🕙 11am-8pm; 🚌 10, 22, 24, 29, 39
Racks of original edgy unisex collections by rising stars in the local fashion world line the walls of this concrete-floored space. Consider making a playful fashion statement with a pair of purple boots from the Hacer Pie line or a leather wallet lined with polka dot fabric. Also see the accessories-focused location on the corner of Defensa and Independencia.

### RUFFINO BAZAR & VINOS *Wine*
☎ 4362-5292; Chacabuco 691; 🕙 9am-6pm Mon-Fri; Ⓜ Line E Belgrano

This cool but crowded wine shop carries a good selection of Argentine bottles plus upscale bar accessories and a variety of imported spirits from pisco to limoncello. Grab a nice Malbec to crack open when you're back home and staring, misty-eyed, at your vacation photos.

### 📖 WALRUS BOOKS *Books*

☎ 4300-7135; www.walrus-books.com.ar; Estados Unidos 617; 🕐 noon-8pm Tue-Sun; 🚌 10, 22, 29, 39, 86

Run out of reading material? This pint-sized bookstore stocks the finest English-language selection in the city. In addition to classics and contemporary literature, there's a small section of Latin American works translated into English – pick up Borges' short stories to get into the swing of things.

# 🍴 EAT

### 🍴 AMICI MIEI *Italian*          $$$

☎ 4362-5562; www.amicimiei.com.ar, in Spanish; Defensa 1072, San Telmo; 🕐 11am-midnight Tue-Sun; 🚌 10, 22, 24, 29

There aren't many places in town where you can dine on gourmet black truffle carpaccio while an impeccably dressed tenor strides through the room crooning 'O Sole Mio.' Try chef Sebastian Rivas Proia's exquisite tagliatelle with shrimp at a charming table for two overlooking Plaza Dorrego.

### 🍴 BRASSERIE PETANQUE
*French*          $$

☎ 4342-7930; www.brasseriepetanque.com; cnr Defensa & Mexico, San Telmo; 🕐 noon-3:30pm & 8:30pm-late Tue-Sun; 🚌 29, 93, 130, 152; ♿ Ⓥ

This bright brasserie is a lively spot for Sunday brunch or a leisurely evening meal. Charismatic waiters pour complimentary aperitifs as you ponder steak tartare or roast chicken and peruse the short but wise list of wines by the glass. The *prix fixe* lunch menu is a steal.

### 🍴 CAFÉ SAN JUAN *Spanish*   $$

☎ 4300-1112; Av San Juan 450, San Telmo; 🕐 noon-4pm & 8:30pm-midnight Tue-Sun; Ⓜ Line C San Juan; Ⓥ

Aside from the gleaming open kitchen, this petite restaurant isn't overly impressive to look at – the focus is firmly on the food at the family-run Café San Juan. A constantly changing chalkboard menu of tapas and main dishes is built around flavorful cheeses, seasonal vegetables like zucchini and eggplant and perfectly al dente pasta.

### 🍴 COMEDOR NIKKAI
*Japanese*          $$

☎ 4300-5848; Av Independencia 732, San Telmo; 🕐 noon-3pm & 8-11pm Mon-Sat; Ⓜ Line C Independencia; Ⓥ

Forget sake cocktails and fashionable clientele – the calm, traditional Comedor Nikkai, tucked away inside the Japanese Association's building, is worlds away from Palermo's stylish eateries. Join a low-key crowd here for steaming bowls of miso and fresh salmon rolls.

### 🍴 EL DESNIVEL *Parrilla*                                     $

☎ 4300-9081; Defensa 855, San Telmo; ⏱ noon-4pm & 8pm-1am Tue-Sun, from 7:30pm Mon; 🚌 10, 22, 24, 29; ♿ ⛴

Eating at dirt-cheap Desnivel is a rite of passage. The convivial *parrilla* atmosphere is buoyed by deadpan waiters, a mix of hungry locals and eager tourists, the skill and speed of the overworked guys on the grill, and – of course – the affordable beef, sizzling *provoleta* (grilled provolone) and fried *empanadas*.

### 🍴 GRAN PARRILLA DEL PLATA *Parrilla*               $$

☎ 4300-8858; cnr Chile & Perú, San Telmo; ⏱ noon-4pm & 8pm-late Mon-Sat, noon-late Sun; 🚌 10, 22, 24, 29; ♿ ⛴

Fancy a chunk of Brie in your salad and a 'real' wine glass? Fine cuts of meat and refined service make this corner *parrilla* a hit with the suits at lunchtime. When the weather's fine, grab a sidewalk table.

### 🍴 LA VINERÍA DE GUALTERIO BOLÍVAR
*Modern Argentine, Spanish*          $$$

☎ 4361-4709; www.lavineriadegual teriobolivar.com, in Spanish; Bolívar 865, San Telmo; ⏱ 1-4pm & 9pm-midnight Tue-Sun; 🚌 10, 22, 24, 29; ♿ V

Furnished in minimalist white and not much larger than a studio apartment, La Vinería feels like a foodie's laboratory – fitting, considering the inventive molecular gastronomy that chef Alejandro Digilio concocts in the open kitchen. His cutting-edge eatery, which offers a nine-course tasting menu paired with several pours of high-end local wines, has attracted international attention since opening in 2007.

### 🍴 MANOLO *Argentine*                                     $

☎ 4307-8743; www.restaurantmanolo .com.ar, in Spanish; cnr Cochabamba & Bolívar, San Telmo; ⏱ noon-1am Tue-Sun; 🚌 10, 22, 24, 29; ♿ ⛴

Honest local cuisine – steaks, salads and a huge menu of Spanish pastas and meat-and-potatoes platters – keep this friendly, family-run corner joint alive and kicking. The budget-friendly prices pull in neighborhood families and groups of hungry boys after *fútbol* practice.

### 🍴 MATILDA'S CAFÉ
*Deli, Cafe*                                                         $

☎ 4300-2216; Chile 673, San Telmo; ⏱ 9am-6pm Mon-Fri; 🚌 10, 22, 24, 29

For delicious chicken Caesar wraps, New York–style bagels, pretty chocolate cupcakes and takeaway cappuccino, swing by Matilda's, one of the newest (and most popular) additions to the neighborhood. The place has a faintly Parisian feel and there are only a handful of seats available; grab one or stroll through San Telmo with your coffee.

### ORIGEN *Organic* $

☎ 4362-7979; cnr Humberto Primo & Perú, San Telmo; ☼ 9am-4pm Mon & Tue, to late Wed-Sun; 🚌 10, 20, 22, 29; ♿ Ⓥ ♨

Flying one of the only organic flags in this part of town, Origen is a bright, relaxed eatery with a short daily menu of fresh dishes like pumpkin ravioli and vegetable stir-fry with ginger. On a sunny day, you'll have to tussle with the locals for an outdoor table.

### PARRILLA 1880 *Parrilla* $

☎ 4307-2746; Defensa 1665; ☼ 12pm-late Tue-Sun; 🚌 10, 29, 39, 152

Locals roll up to this no-frills *parrilla* for juicy cuts of steak, spicy chorizo, garlic-and-parsley-topped french fries, green salads and red wine served in *pingüinos* (penguin-shaped pitchers.) It's located across the street from Parque Lezama – an area that's a bit sketchy after dark – so jump in a taxi if it's late.

### SAGARDI EUSKAL TABERNA *Basque* $$$

☎ 4361-2538; www.sagardi.com.ar; Humberto Primo 319, San Telmo; ☼ noon-4pm & 8pm-midnight; 🚌 10, 22, 24, 29; ♿ Ⓥ

This cavernous, striking Basque eatery heralds San Telmo's gentrification. Swing by in the evening to

Brunch at bright Brasserie Petanque (p76)

pile your plate high with savory tapas and try the house *tempranillo* at the gorgeous, oversized communal wooden table in the front room.

### TABERNA BASKA *Basque* $$

☎ 4334-0903; Chile 980; ⏰ noon-3:30pm & 8pm-late Tue-Sat, noon-3:30pm Sun; Ⓜ Line C Independencia
This long-standing, brightly lit Basque restaurant serves up down-home classics like *jamón iberico* and piping-hot paella to a crowd nostalgic for their Spanish mothers.

## DRINK

### 647 *Bar, Restaurant*

☎ 4331-3026; www.club647.com; Tacuarí 647, San Telmo; ⏰ 8pm-late Mon-Sat; Ⓜ Line C Independencia
This lavish Shanghai-style lounge boasts a talented barman and an experimental cocktail menu (try anything involving lychee fruit, but skip the margarita.) After-dinner drinks here are no bargain, especially by San Telmo standards, but shelling out the pesos is worth it for the chance to feel like a rock star in a space that feels like an otherwordly opium den.

### BAR BRITÁNICO *Cafe, Bar*

☎ 4361-2107; cnr Brasil & Defensa, San Telmo; ⏰ 24hr except midnight Mon-8am Tue; 🚌 10, 29, 39, 152;

A classic corner cafe on the edge of Parque Lezama (p72), Bar Británico has an evocative old wooden interior and big glass windows that open to the street. Drop in for a *café cortado* (small espresso with milk) in the morning or a beer on a sunny afternoon.

### BAR PLAZA DORREGO *Cafe, Bar*

☎ 4361-0141; cnr Defensa & Humberto Primo; ⏰ 8am-3am; 🚌 24, 29, 130, 152; 🍷
Despite the constant tourist presence, Bar Plaza Dorrego remains one of BA's most atmospheric watering holes. Take a load off to observe the tired but tuxedoed waiters making their rounds through an interior cluttered with antique bottles. Outdoors, backpackers knock back beer at rickety tables littered with peanut shells.

### BAR SEDDÓN *Cafe, Bar*

☎ 4342-3700; cnr Chile & Defensa, San Telmo; ⏰ 9am-4am Sun-Fri, 6pm-4am Sat; 🚌 24, 29, 130, 152
This laid-back bar is outfitted with black-and-white tiles, rustic wood tables and the glow of hundreds of candles, and is housed in an old pharmacy. Drop in for an icy *chopp* (glass of draught beer) or for a late-night glass of red – you'll keep good company with a neighborhood crowd.

## LEARNING LUNFARDO

Hearing some phrases on the street that your teacher never covered in Spanish 101? Forget looking them up in your pocket dictionary – you're hearing Lunfardo, a local dialect that developed in the early 20th century with influences ranging from jail slang and gaucho speak to the mishmash of languages spoken by French, Portuguese and Italian immigrants. The dialect was occasionally used in classic tango music, and today the language continues to thrive and grow – if you're listening for it, you'll hear 'Che, boludo' (a casual form of address between friends, or alternatively, an insult) several times a day. Brush up on local lingo by mastering a few key words and phrases:

> *Pibe* – boy
> *Bondi* – bus
> *Re-copado* (adjective) and *una masa* (noun) – very cool
> *Que burra* – What a gorgeous woman
> *Ni en pedo* – I wouldn't do it even if I were drunk

### ▮ DOPPELGÄNGER
*Bar, Restaurant*

☎ 4300-0201; www.doppelganger.com.ar; cnr Av Juan de Garay & Bolívar, San Telmo; ✆ 7pm-late Tue-Fri, 8pm-late Sat; Ⓜ Line C San Juan; ♿

Mark our words: this cool, calm, emerald-hued corner bar is one of the only places in Capital Federal where you can count on a perfectly mixed martini. That's because Doppelgänger, in homage to an immigrant tradition from the 1940s, specializes in vermouth cocktails. Channel Don Draper by ordering an old-fashioned.

### ▮ EL FEDERAL *Cafe, Bar*

☎ 4300-4313; cnr Perú & Carlos Calvo, San Telmo; ✆ 8am-2am Mon-Thu, 8am-4am Fri-Sun; 🚌 10, 20, 29, 86; ♿

El Federal's decorative wooden bar and old-fashioned cash registers are trappings of days gone by – the well-loved corner joint has been serving huge sandwiches and *cerveza artesanal* (hand-crafted beer) under the glow of yellow lamplight since 1864. Also check out the newer La Poesía, El Federal's literary-themed sister bar, on the corner of Chile and Bolívar.

### ▮ GIBRALTAR *Bar, Restaurant*

☎ 4362-5310; Perú 895, San Telmo; ✆ 6pm-4am Mon-Fri, noon-4am Sat & Sun; 🚌 10, 20, 29, 86

Porteños and expats hit this English-style pub for icy pints, pool tables, juicy burgers and excellent ethnic dishes. Line up at the bar to ask for a bowl of Thai curry and a frosted glass of whatever's on tap.

### Stella Torres Botía
*Colombian transplant to Buenos Aires; co-owner of Doppelgänger Bar*

**Your bar must be the only place in the city that doesn't serve beer.**
Probably! Traditionally, porteños (Buenos Aires locals) don't drink a lot of cocktails, but lately we're seeing a slow movement in Buenos Aires towards martinis and aperitifs. **Why martinis?** Vermouth was popular with immigrants who came to Argentina from Europe in the '40s and '50s. Today, when locals who don't know much about cocktails come in, we encourage them to try something classic. Our best seller is the old-fashioned. **Where else do you go for drinks in San Telmo?** La Puerta Roja (p82) for a beer, Gibraltar (opposite) for whiskey – just get there early enough to beat the crowd. **And in the rest of the city?** Gran Bar Danzon (p98) has an excellent selection of wines by the glass. **Any dining recommendations?** I regularly eat at Parrilla 1880 (p78). Sagardi (p78) is great for a quick bite, or go to Comedor Nikkai (p76) for sushi.

### ☎ LA PUERTA ROJA *Bar*
☎ 4362-5649; Chacabuco 733, San Telmo; ⏰ 6am-6am; Ⓜ Line C Independencia

A young crowd of pub crawlers and neighborhood kids climb the stairs to socialize and get sloshed at La Puerto Roja (the Red Door). This is a proper bar – no sweet cocktails or chalkboard wine list here – you'll be having a cold beer, vodka on the rocks or scotch, straight up.

### ☎ PRIDE CAFÉ *Gay Cafe, Bar*
☎ 4300-6435; Balcarce 869, San Telmo; ⏰ 9am-9pm Mon-Fri, 11am-10pm Sat, 10am-8pm Sun; 🚌 10, 22, 29, 86; ♿

This cheerful, gay-friendly cafe serves up inexpensive breakfasts (think *dulce de leche* liqueur-smothered crepes and banana smoothies) to an eclectic crowd. Grab an Argentine fashion magazine and ask for the mouth-watering *limonada con gengibre* (lemonade with ginger).

## ⭐ PLAY

### ⭐ BAR SUR *Tango*
☎ 4362-6086; www.bar-sur.com.ar; cnr Estados Unidos & Balcarce, San Telmo; ⏰ 8pm-late; 🚌 10, 22, 29, 86

Historic Bar Sur is one of the city's most celebrated, intimate (and expensive) tango show venues: you'll pay handsomely to sip champagne

at one of a dozen tables. Be prepared – the upscale dinner show is often participatory – so avoid it if you're not prepared to try a few tangled steps.

### ⭐ CENTRO CULTURAL TORQUATO TASSO
*Tango, Live Music*

☎ 4307-6506; www.torquatotasso .com.ar, in Spanish; Defensa 1575, San Telmo; ⏰ shows 10pm Tue-Sat; 🚌 10, 22, 93, 130

Serious tango musicians, both established and up-and-coming, perform at this well-respected venue just off Parque Lezama.

---

> ## HISTORIC BAR HOP
>
> The city of Buenos Aires officially recognizes 54 bars *(bares notables)* as points of historic interest. For a healthy dose of porteño-style nostalgia, grab a friend – or a good book – and go on a historic bar hop through San Telmo, Congreso and the Microcentro.
>
> Start with a coffee and *medialuna* (croissant) with a view of Parque Lezama at Bar Británico (p79), then head to El Federal (p80) for monster-sized sandwiches and a colorful pitcher of *clericot* (a sangria-like drink made with fruit and wine.) Play the tourist with hot chocolate and churros at Café Tortoni (p43), then continue to the classy New Brighton (p44) for cocktail hour. Finish with an icy *chopp* (beer) and a lively crowd at Bar Seddón (p79).

## ⭐ EL QUERANDÍ *Tango*

☎ 4345-1770; www.querandi.com.ar; Perú 302, Montserrat; 🕑 dinner 8pm, show 10pm; Ⓜ Line E Bolívar; ♿

By day, El Querandí is an upscale restaurant serving salmon to businessmen – by night, the space is completely blackened for its famous tango dinner shows. These are stylish, slick, sexy and profes-sional. And very popular – bookings essential.

## ⭐ EL VIEJO ALMACÉN
*Tango*

☎ 4307-7388; www.viejo-almacen. com.ar, in Spanish; cnr Balcarce & Av Independencia, San Telmo; 🕑 dinner from 8pm, show 10pm; 🚌 10, 29, 93 130, 152; ♿

This polished tango show, put on nightly in one of San Telmo's old colonial homes, incorporates in-digenous music and dance to the usual routine. It's widely consid-ered one of the best shows in the city – but avoid dining at the ge-neric restaurant of the same name, located just across the street.

## ⭐ LA CUMPARSITA
*Tango, Live Music*

☎ 4361-6880; www.lacumparsitatango .com.ar; Chile 302, San Telmo; 🕑 8pm-late; 🚌 10, 22, 29, 86, 126

This low-key tango bar hosts a legion of excellent musicians and vocalists, dancing duos, and an appealing mix of locals and tourists coming in from the street to drink wine in the intimate wood-paneled space.

## ⭐ LA TRASTIENDA *Live Music*

☎ 4342-7650; www.latrastienda.com, in Spanish; Balcarce 460, San Telmo; admission prices vary; 🕑 from 6pm Mon-Sun; 🚌 24, 29, 86, 130; ♿

This happening live-music venue hosts acts from Latin America and beyond – highly anticipated gigs have included Damien Rice, Kevin Johansen and the Nada, Bright Eyes and Argentine-born indie darling José Gonzalez. The theater has standing room for up to 1000 downstairs and another 350 seats on the upper level.

## ⭐ MUSEUM *Dance Club*

☎ 4771-9628; www.museumclub.com .ar, in Spanish; Perú 535, San Telmo; 🕑 8pm-2am Wed, 10pm-late Fri-Sun; Ⓜ Line E Belgrano; ♿

The striking steel building that houses Museum was designed by Gustave Eiffel (yes, the same French architect who made an indelible mark on the Parisian skyline), though what transpires inside isn't quite as romantic – on Wednesday nights, the dark, lofty interior is a full-blown meat market as the macho 'after office' crowds loosen their ties and get rowdy over strong cocktails.

# >LA BOCA

Any student of the Spanish language can translate the name of this rough-and-tumble southern neighborhood: La Boca means 'the mouth,' a reference to the barrio's location at the mouth of the Riachuelo. The working-class Italian immigrants who settled around the port during the mid-19th century left a powerful legacy – they 'borrowed' ship paint to decorate their ramshackle houses, creating the vibrantly hued stretch now known as Caminito, and, along with their neighboring Spaniards, Africans and gauchos, they invented tango. Today, many porteños (BA locals) avoid La Boca, criticizing its dirty river, dangerous side streets and the violent *futból* fans who frequent La Bombonera stadium. But La Boca is on the upswing – the cutting-edge Proa art gallery has undergone a major renovation, and foreigners still flock here to see the colorful houses and campy tango performers. The tourist spectacle can be cheesy, and the neighborhood surrounding Caminito isn't safe to wander around, especially at night. But the old port and the city's south hold a certain romance that didn't escape tango composers like Fernando Solanas, who wrote 'I carry the South like a destiny of my heart/I am from the South like the melodies of the *bandoneón*.'

---

## LA BOCA

### 🅞 SEE
Caminito ....................... 1 B5
Fundación Proa ............. 2 B5
Museo de Bellas Artes de La
   Boca Benito
   Quinquela Martín ...... 3 C5
Museo de la Pasión
   Boquense ................... 4 B4

### 🅐 SHOP
Centro Cultural de los
   Artistas ....................... 5 B5

### 🍴 EAT
El Obrero ........................ 6 C3
Il Matterello .................. 7 B4

### ⭐ PLAY
La Bombonera Estadio
   (Alberto J Armando) .. 8 B4

# ◉ SEE

## ◉ CAMINITO

🚌 29, 64; ♿

La Boca's most famous street is a tangle of brightly painted houses, local artists selling splashy paintings of BA's tourist sites, and flashy tango dancers twirling for a camera-snapping audience. The surrounding stalls offer generally high-quality crafts (with prices to match). Also see p18.

## ◉ FUNDACIÓN PROA

☎ 4104-1000; www.proa.org; Av Don Pedro de Mendoza 1929, La Boca; admission $10; ⏱ 11am-7pm Tue-Sun; 🚌 29, 53, 64, 152; ♿

After a well-executed renovation, this contemporary art gallery and foundation is almost too cool for La Boca. Each year, Proa hosts six temporary shows from Argentina and abroad, as well as workshops, courses, conferences and concerts. The sophisticated cafe on the top level stands in high contrast to the surrounding barrio. See also p18.

## ◉ MUSEO DE BELLAS ARTES DE LA BOCA BENITO QUINQUELA MARTÍN

☎ 4301-1080; Av Don Pedro de Mendoza 1835, La Boca; admission $2; ⏱ 10am-5pm Tue-Fri, 11am-5:30pm Sat & Sun, closed Jan; 🚌 29, 64, 152; ♿

Argentine painter Benito Quinquela Martín (1890–1977) lived and

### MAGIC BUS

So you want to go on an authentic city bus tour (the kind that's free of air conditioning and camera-wielding tourists?) Depart from La Boca on public bus 29 – the main stop is at the bottom of El Caminito – for an unforgettable ride through the city with a colorful cast of local characters and a moody bus driver at the helm. The rusty *colectivo* (bus) leaves La Boca and barrels through San Telmo (p70), around the Casa Rosada (p38), along Av de Mayo to Av 9 de Julio and right by the Obelisco (p40), then past the imposing Palacio de las Aguas Corrientes (p54). After the bumpy ride, you'll want to get off at Plaza Italia in Palermo and head to a park for some peace and quiet or to one of Palermo Viejo's cool eateries for drinks and dinner.

worked in this huge, boxy waterfront building before donating it to the government in 1936; these days, the structure houses a museum showing the work of national artists like Berni and Soldi, and, more significantly, an outstanding collection of Martín's own colorfully painted depictions of La Boca.

## ◉ MUSEO DE LA PASIÓN BOQUENSE

☎ 4362-1100; www.museoboquense .com, in Spanish; Brandsen 805, La Boca; admission $28; ⏱ 10am-6pm, closed on game days; 🚌 10, 29, 64; ♿

No visit to La Boca is complete without visiting this slick museum

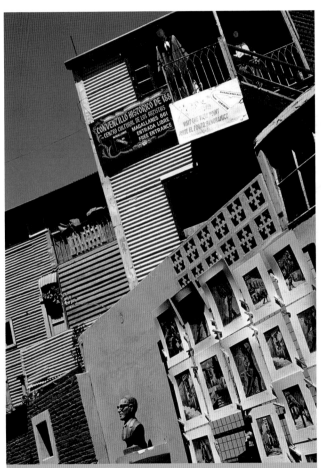

Don't miss the colorful world of the Caminito

and shrine to the Boca Juniors football club. Petrified of braving the volatile stadium crowds? Step inside a giant soccer ball, where a 360-degree movie screen transports you into a crowd-filled stadium – not as exciting as the real thing, but close.

# SHOP

## ☐ CENTRO CULTURAL DE LOS ARTISTAS *Art, Handicrafts*

☎ 4301-1080; Magallanes 861, La Boca; ⏲ 10am-6pm; 🚌 29, 64

While the area around El Caminito is jammed with dozens of markets and shops hawking crafts and souvenirs, this complex was the first and remains the best. Not only does it give you an opportunity to peek inside one of the former tenements, but it also has a small art gallery where you can buy local paintings.

# ᵂᴵ EAT

## ᵂᴵ EL OBRERO *Parrilla $*

☎ 4362-9912; www.bodegonelobrero. com.ar; Agustín Caffarena 64, La Boca; ⏲ noon-4pm & 8pm-midnight Mon-Sat; 🚌 29, 64, 86, 130; ♿

Ironically, the exterior of BA's most famous *bodegón* (workers' cafe; *obrero* translates as workers or working-class) is often illuminated by the flash of paparazzi bulbs as local celebrities pull up for high-profile dinners of roasted

ribs and *milanesa* (fried steak). If your limo doesn't arrive after dinner, don't be tempted to walk – take a taxi, La Boca's a tough 'hood.

## ᵂᴵ IL MATTERELLO *Italian $$*

☎ 4307-0529; Martín Rodríguez 517, La Boca; ⏲ 12:30-3pm & 8:30pm-midnight Tue-Sat, 12:30-3pm Sun, closed Jan; 🚌 29, 64, 86, 152; ♿

This simple, attractively furnished La Boca eatery specializes in home-made pastas tossed with classic Italian sauces like *carbonara* and *puttanesca*. The service is spotty, but the tiramisú is delicious.

### THE EMPANADA TRAIL

First prize for fantastic and fuss-free finger food goes to Argentina. *Empanadas*, baked (or sometimes fried) pastries stuffed with meat or cheese, are the go-to snack for *porteños* – when they're having a few friends over for drinks, they'll order a box from the local *empanadería*. The shape of each pastry is cleverly chosen to indicate the filling inside; the most popular pockets are *carne* (minced meat), *carne picante* (spicy minced meat), *cebolla y queso* (onion and cheese), *jamón y queso* (ham and cheese), *humita* (creamed corn) and *caprese* (tomato, basil, and mozzarella.) Packing a picnic? Just look for an *empanadería* that's busy with locals – *porteños* are fanatical about where they buy these savory specialties.

## DIEGO ARMANDO MARADONA

In recent years, he's made the headlines for drug addiction and heart attacks, but back in his glory days, Diego Armando Maradona was the populist hero of Argentina. Along with Brazilian Pelé, Maradona's considered the greatest *fútbol* (soccer) player ever to grace the turf. Born in 1960 in a Buenos Aires shantytown, Diego made his professional debut for Argentinos Juniors in 1976 at the age of 15. He transferred to his favorite club, Boca Juniors, in 1981, finally ending up with SSC Napoli (and making a record salary) in 1984. But it was playing for Argentina that made Maradona a superstar. His two goals in the World Cup quarter-final against England in 1986 are legendary football moments. With the first, he surreptitiously punched the ball into goal, later claiming it was 'La Mano de Dios' ('The Hand of God') that helped him. With the second goal, Diego bamboozled the entire English defense in what was later named the 'Goal of the Century.' Maradona left Napoli in 1992, after a 15-month ban for failing a drug test for cocaine, and was sent home from the 1994 World Cup for testing positive to ephedrine. Though his health issues have made the news in recent years, he displayed high energy (an understatement?) while coaching the national team at 2010's World Cup in South Africa.

# PLAY

## LA BOMBONERA *Sport*

☎ 4362-2260; www.bocajuniors.com
.ar, in Spanish; Estadio Alberto J Armando
(La Bombonera), Brandsen 805, La Boca;
admission free on non-game days;
🕐 varies, check website for details;
🚌 29, 64, 86, 152

Watching a football game at this La Boca stadium is an experience. The stands are so rickety that the whole thing rocks when fans jump up and down, singing songs of abuse to the other side. Consider venturing toward the Boca Juniors' home turf through a tour operator like Tangol (www.tangol .com) – matches can be more than a little unruly. See also p12.

# >RECOLETA & BARRIO NORTE

Old money abounds in Recoleta. The city's wealthiest citizens relocated here as the yellow fever epidemic ravaged San Telmo in 1871, and this north-of-center area developed to suit the refined tastes of the Spanish elite. Many members of the original high society never left the neighborhood – they're buried in grand fashion in the magnificent Cementerio de la Recoleta, and their aesthetic contributions live on. This is the city's most Parisian quarter, featuring wide avenues, belle-epoque apartment buildings and beautifully landscaped parks. Swanky Av Alvear is dripping with diamonds – opulent hotels like the Alvear Place roll out the red carpet for distinguished guests while exclusive boutiques sell sapphires to rich porteñas (BA locals) toting tiny dogs. While Recoleta's natives are a conservative set, a more diverse population streams out of bookstores and ice-cream shops on Av Santa Fe in nearby Barrio Norte, where dozens of old mansions have been converted into restaurants and bars.

## RECOLETA & BARRIO NORTE

### ● SEE
Basílica de Nuestra
    Señora del Pilar ..........1  D2
Biblioteca Nacional ......2  C1
Cementerio de la
    Recoleta ....................3  D2
Centro Cultural
    Recoleta ....................4  D2
Daniel Abate ................5  B2
Floralis Genérica ..........6  D1
Isabel Anchorena ........7  F3
Museo Nacional de
    Bellas Artes ..............8  D1
Museo Xul Solar ..........9  B3
Palais de Glace ..........10  E1
Praxis ........................11  E3

### ◐ SHOP
Airedelsur ..................12  E2
A.Y. Not Dead ............13  F3

Buenos Aires Design ....14  D2
El Ateneo Grand
    Splendid ..................15  D4
El Fenix ......................16  F4
Feria de Artesanos
    de Plaza Francia ......17  D1
Josefina Ferroni ..........18  F3
Patio Bullrich ............19  F2
Rossi & Caruso ..........20  E4
Tealosophy ................21  E2
Tramando ..................22  E2
Wussman Shop ..........23  E3

### ⑪ EAT
788 Food Bar ............24  D3
Cumaná ....................25  D4
Gran Bar Danzon ......26  F3
La Bourgogne ............27  E2
L'Orangerie ..........(see 27)
Oviedo ......................28  B3

### ▼ DRINK
Buller Pub & Brewery ..29  D2
Clásica y Moderna ......30  D4
La Biela ......................31  E2
Milión ........................32  E4

### ★ PLAY
Basement Club ..........33  D3
Glam ..........................34  A4
Notorious ..................35  D4

# ◉ SEE

## ◉ BASÍLICA DE NUESTRA SEÑORA DEL PILAR

☎ 4803-6793; www.basilicadelpilar
.org.ar, in Spanish; Junín 1904, Recoleta;
admission free; ⏱ 8am-9pm; 🚌 10, 17,
60, 92, 110; ♿

Yes, that's a pair of skulls on your right as you enter the basilica. But the centerpiece of this gleaming white colonial church, built by Jesuits in 1716, is a Peruvian altar adorned with silver from Argentina's northwest. The crypt leads into underground tunnels that once connected the basilica to other sections of the city. Free tours in English and Spanish start at 10:30am and 6:15pm Monday to Saturday.

## ◉ BIBLIOTECA NACIONAL

☎ 4808-6000; www.bn.gov.ar, in Spanish; Agüero 2502, Recoleta; admission free; ⏱ 9am-8pm Mon-Fri, noon-7pm Sat & Sun; 🚌 10, 21, 37, 38, 41, 59, 60, 93, 110; ♿

Sixties-style concrete meets futuristic design at the imposing National Library, conceived by famed architect Clorinda Testa and standing on the site where Eva and Juan Perón once lived. Evita died here in 1952, and the home was later razed by the post-

Check out the street art at Centro Cultural Recoleta

## LITTLE EVA

The short life of the iconic Eva María Duarte de Perón was like a Cinderella story with a dark twist of an ending. The small-town girl left home at the tender age of 15 and moved to the big city, where she worked, and often struggled to make ends meet, as a radio actress. At 24, she met Juan Perón, a politician twice her age, at a fundraiser. Their fast and furious courtship culminated with Perón's election to the Argentine presidency in 1946. As the nation's charismatic first lady, Evita (little Eva) was a feminist and philanthropist who campaigned tirelessly for the city's poor. The porteño working class adored her, though her critics often point to the sharp contrast between her political platform and her glamorous, European-designer-label-wearing image. Eva had bigger problems to contend with, however, as the public denounced the president's dictatorial style, the military staged a coup against her husband, and, to top it off, she was diagnosed with cancer. Evita died at age 33, and while she remains a tragic character in foreigners' imaginations, the local perception of the Perón legacy is darker and more complex, wrapped up in the memory of the bloody political and social events that followed Eva's premature death.

Perón government, but a stylized statue at the foot of the hill pays tribute to the former first lady.

### ⊙ CEMENTERIO DE LA RECOLETA

☎ 4803-1594; www.cementeriorecoleta.com.ar; Junín 1790, Recoleta; admission free; ⏲ 7am-6pm, check blackboard for free English tour times; 🚌 10, 17, 60, 92, 110; ♿

Visitors come to this famous cemetery to make the pilgrimage to Evita's tomb, but the labyrinthine necropolis is a destination in itself. Explore the final resting place of some of the country's most influential figures – politicians, educators, artists – with a tour guide, or just get lost among the stray cats and cobwebs of the cemetery's shadowy passageways. See also p11.

### ⊙ CENTRO CULTURAL RECOLETA

☎ 4803-1040; www.centrocultural recoleta.org, in Spanish; Junín 1930, Recoleta; admission by donation; ⏲ 2-9pm Mon-Fri, 10am-9pm Sat & Sun; 🚌 10, 17, 60, 92, 110; ♿

Sandwiched between Buenos Aires Design (p95) and the Basílica de Nuestra Señora del Pilar (opposite), this one-time Franciscan convent is now one of the city's most dynamic cultural centers. The spacious rooms and old-fashioned archways make a picturesque setting for excellent sculpture, photography and video exhibits, while the sweeping terrace hosts live jazz performances.

## GALLERY WALK

Upscale Recoleta is the epicenter of the city's art scene. If you fancy a little hobnobbing with porteño painters and the rich patrons who support them – while sipping free champagne, of course – keep your eye out for events and openings at these galleries.

> **Daniel Abate** (☎ 4804-8247; www.danielabategaleria.com.ar; Pasaje Bollini 2170; ☽ noon-7pm Tue-Sat) Edgy, youthful visual arts exhibits in an unpretentious setting.

> **Isabel Anchorena** (☎ 4811-5335; www.galeriaisabelanchorena.sion.com; Arenales 1239; ☽ 11am-8pm Mon-Fri & 11am-1pm Sat) This old-school gallery represents dozens of talents in the realm of sculpture, photography and painting.

> **Praxis** (☎ 4813-8639; www.praxis-art.com; Arenales 1311; ☽ 10:30am-8pm Mon-Fri & 10:30am-2pm Sat) Contemporary Latin American art with an international reach – Praxis also has spaces in Miami and New York.

### ⊙ FLORALIS GENÉRICA

**Plaza Naciones Unidas, Recoleta;** 🚌 **12, 124, 130;** ♿

This gargantuan solar-powered flower sculpture is the inspired creation of architect Eduardo Catalano, who designed and funded the project in 2002. Check out the stunning Floralis Genérica at dawn, when its enormous metallic petals open to the sun, or at dusk, when the flower delicately closes for the night.

### ⊙ MUSEO NACIONAL DE BELLAS ARTES

☎ 4803-8814; www.mnba.org.ar; Av Del Libertador 1473, Recoleta; admission free; ☽ 12:30-8:30pm Tue-Fri, 9:30am-8:30pm Sat & Sun; 🚌 17, 67, 92, 93, 130; ♿

The country's most important fine-arts museum boasts an extensive collection of 19th- and 20th-century Argentine and indigenous art, as well as works by European masters such as Renoir, Rodin, Monet, Toulouse-Lautrec, Gauguin, Rembrandt and Van Gogh.

### ⊙ MUSEO XUL SOLAR

☎ 4824-3302; www.xulsolar.org.ar; Laprida 1212, Recoleta; admission $10; ☽ noon-7:30pm Tue-Fri, noon-7pm Sat Ⓜ Line D Agüero

How could you *not* be curious about a man who created his own language and claimed to live in his own private time zone? This museum exhibits the unusual artwork and inventions of the avant-garde painter, musician, writer and mathematician Alejandro Xul Solar (1887–1963). A friend of Borges, he dabbled in fields as diverse as astrology and philosophy.

### ⊙ PALAIS DE GLACE

**www.palaisdeglace.org, in Spanish; Posadas 1725, Recoleta; admission free, tours & exhibits $10;** ⏱ **noon-8pm Tue-Fri, 10am-8pm Sat & Sun** 🚍 **17, 61, 92, 93, 130;** ♿

The name (and circular shape) give it away – the Palais de Glace was once the ice-skating rink of BA's high society. The glamorous belle-epoque structure, built in 1910, also served as a tango ballroom before being declared a National Monument in 2004. Now the landmark building exhibits visual arts; on weekend afternoons, guided tours of the building (in English) start at 5pm (bookings required).

# 🛍 SHOP

### ⊡ AIREDELSUR
*Home Decor, Handicrafts*

☎ **4803-6100; www.airedelsur.com; Av Alvear 1833 #1129, Recoleta;** ⏱ **10am-8pm Mon-Fri, 10am-2pm Sat;** 🚍 **17, 59, 67, 75, 102**

The rustic chic airedelsur label was beloved by porteños long before it was featured in *Vogue*. Designer Marcelo Lucini collaborates with Argentine craftsmen to create stunningly original home decor made with alpaca silver, wood, onyx and other all-natural materials. Queen Rania of Jordan reportedly picked up more than 200 pieces for her palaces.

### ⊡ A.Y. NOT DEAD *Fashion*

☎ **4815-7954; www.aynotdead.com.ar; Posadas 1220, Recoleta;** ⏱ **11am-7pm Mon-Sat;** 🚍 **17, 59, 67, 75, 102**

Half street, half punk, A.Y. Not Dead always makes a splash at BA's bi-annual Fashion Week (p25). Peruse the edgy collection of weathered denim skinny jeans, graphic jersey tanks and rainbow-hued vinyl miniskirts at the Recoleta branch of this youthful fashion house.

### ⊡ BUENOS AIRES DESIGN
*Home Decor, Design*

☎ **5777-6000; www.designrecoleta.com.ar; Av Pueyrredón 2501, Recoleta;** ⏱ **10am-9pm;** 🚍 **10, 17, 60, 92, 110**

This chic contemporary design center bustles with dozens of stores specializing in minimalist furniture, high-tech lighting and sophisticated home decor. Pop into the airy Morph boutique for snazzy wine decanters and leather breakfast trays.

### ⊡ EL ATENEO GRAND SPLENDID
*Books, Music*

☎ **4813-6052; Av Santa Fe 1860, Recoleta;** ⏱ **9am-10pm Mon-Sat, noon-10pm Sun;** Ⓜ **Line D Callao**

Though part of the El Ateneo chain, this is no ordinary bookstore – the Grand Splendid occupies a fabulous antique cinema and theater where Carlos Gardel, Argentina's

El Ateneo Grand Splendid (p95), possibly the most spectacular bookshop in the world

iconic tango legend, crooned on stage to an adoring crowd. Today, bookshelves crowd the mezzanine. Relive the theatrical magic with coffee on the 1920s-style stage.

### EL FENIX *Wine, Deli*
☎ 4811-0363; Av Santa Fe 1199, Retiro; ⏰ 8am-8pm Mon-Fri, 8am-2pm Sat; 🚌 10, 21, 39, 67, 152

An excellent city wine shop. Name your preferences and price range, then put the knowledgeable staff to the test.

### FERIA DE ARTESANOS DE PLAZA FRANCIA *Market*
www.feriaplazafrancia.com; Plaza Francia, Recoleta; ⏰ 11am-8pm Sat & Sun; 🚌 10, 17, 60, 92, 110

On sunny weekend afternoons, this upscale craft market teems with artisans selling exquisite bronze jewelry, brightly colored cotton sundresses and hand-woven clutch purses. The sprawling display enlivens the green slope of Plaza Francia.

### JOSEFINA FERRONI *Shoes*
☎ 5811-1951; www.josefinaferroni .com.ar; Arenales 1278, Recoleta; ⏰ 2-8pm Mon, 11am-8pm Tue-Sat; 🚌 10, 21, 39, 67, 152

Argentina's answer to Jimmy Choo. The old-school glamour and coquettish colors of these gorgeously crafted boots, platform heels and open-toed flats have earned Josefina Ferroni countless porteña fans and growing international exposure.

## 🏬 PATIO BULLRICH
*Shopping Mall*

☎ 4814-7400/7500; www.shopping bullrich.com.ar; Av del Libertador 750, Recoleta; ☽ 10am-9pm; 🚌 17, 61, 62, 92, 124, 130

Patio Bullrich is the place where posh porteños part with their pesos; expect international luxury brands like Salvatore Ferragamo alongside exclusive local design shops and upscale cafes.

## 🏬 ROSSI & CARUSO *Leather*

☎ 4811-1538; www.rossicaruso.com; Av Santa Fe 1601, Recoleta; ☽ 9:30am-8pm Mon-Fri, 10am-7pm Sat; 🚌 17, 59, 67, 75, 102

Should you be in the market for a fine leather saddle or a serious gaucho knife, you've come to the right place. The leather goods

here, from knee-high riding boots to belts and bags, are beautifully made.

## 🏬 TRAMANDO
*Fashion, Home Decor*

☎ 4811-0465; www.tramando .com; Rodríguez Peña 1973, Recoleta; ☽ 10:30am-8:30pm Mon-Fri, 11am-7pm Sat; 🚌 17, 59, 67, 92

Designer Martín Churba is a highly respected name on the local and international fashion circuit. His lighthearted, eco-friendly collection plays with pattern, texture, stamping, recycled fabrics and the occasional indigenous textile.

## 🏬 WUSSMANN SHOP
*Paper, Stationery*

☎ 4811-2444; www.wussmannshop. com.ar; Rodriguez Peña 1399, Recoleta; ☽ 10:30am-8pm Mon-Fri; 11am-2pm Sat; 🚌 10, 39, 59, 152

## TEA FOR TWO

Following in the grand tradition of Londoners and society ladies, porteñas have taken to the ritual of afternoon tea. Which isn't to say that *mate* is on its way out, mind you – taking a break for chamomile and crumpets is just another excuse for these highly social souls to get together and discuss whether or not the president has had plastic surgery. If you're short on time, pick up the trendiest tea leaves in town at the charming **Tealosophy** ( ☎ 4804-7020; www.tealosophy.com; Av Alvear 1883 #37; ☽ 10:30am-8pm Mon-Sat). Have an hour or two to spare? Take your tea in style at the lavish **L'Orangerie** ( ☎ 4808-2949; www.alvearpalace.com; Alvear Palace Hotel, Av Alvear 1891; ☽ 4:30pm Mon-Sat & 5pm Sun), where white-gloved service and impossibly elegant little cakes await guests fond of old-fashioned pleasantries.

Writers and artists delight in the gorgeous handmade paper at this chic stationery shop. Leatherbound journals, monogrammed stationery, and oversized sketchbooks are made with recycled paper; come for one-of-a-kind invitations or hand-painted wrapping paper.

# EAT

## 788 FOOD BAR
*Modern Argentine* $$

☎ 4814-4788; www.788food-bar.com.ar, in Spanish; Arenales 1877, Barrio Norte; 🕙 10am-2am Mon-Sat; Ⓜ Line D Callao; 🚌 10, 39, 60; Ⓥ &

Foodies and cocktail connoisseurs alike rave about 788 Food Bar: an insulated bread box is delivered to your table on arrival, the fusion cuisine is simple and gourmet and the mixed drinks served in the upstairs lounge are superb. Best of all is the (reverse) sticker shock: the set lunch menu hardly costs more than a taxi ride across town.

## CUMANÁ
*Northern Argentine* $

☎ 4813-9207; Rodriguez Peña 1149, Recoleta; 🕙 noon-1am; 🚌 10, 39, 152; & Ⓥ &

This bright, upbeat eatery is one of the only places in town serving traditional dishes from far-flung provinces of Argentina. The hearty *criollo* (Spanish/Indian) cuisine baking in the adobe oven includes

*locro,* a thick corn-based stew made with meat and vegetables. Don't miss the *humita,* a creamy cheese and corn mixture wrapped up in corncob leaves.

## GRAN BAR DANZON
*International* $$

☎ 4811-1108; www.granbardanzon.com.ar; Libertad 1161, Retiro; 🕙 7pm-late, from 8pm Sat & Sun; 🚌 10, 39, 67, 102, 152; Ⓥ

Gran Bar Danzon is the kind of place you drop by with the intention of trying a glass of wine or two with friends – but thanks to the cool urban atmosphere, you're still there four hours later, sampling sushi and confit of duck and pretending not to stare at the parade of pretty people squeezing past your table.

## LA BOURGOGNE
*French* $$$

☎ 4808-2100; www.alvearpalace.com; Alvear Palace Hotel, Av Alvear 1891, Recoleta; 🕙 noon-3:30pm & 7:30pm-midnight Mon-Sat; 🚌 67, 93, 130; &

This cultivated, classy French restaurant at the Alvear Palace Hotel sees sommeliers gliding through hushed rooms as chef Jean Paul Bondoux creates courses and set menus centered on caviar, fish and rabbit. The adjacent Taste Vins cellar also hosts wine tastings (p16).

## OVIEDO *Spanish* $$$

☎ 4822-5415; www.oviedoresto.com
.ar, in Spanish; Beruti 2602, Barrio Norte;
⏰ noon-3:30pm, 8pm-1am; Ⓜ Line D
Pueyrredón; Ⓥ

The sole and sea bass at Oviedo
are so fresh they're practically still
flopping around. Prepared with
contemporary Spanish flair and
paired with cold white wine, fish
takes center stage at this fine dining institution –although melt-in-
your-mouth pork dishes are also
worth writing home about.

# Ⓨ DRINK

## Ⓨ BULLER PUB & BREWERY
*Bar*

☎ 4808-9061; www.bullerpub
.com; Roberto M Ortiz 1827, Recoleta;
⏰ noon-late; 🚌 17, 61, 62, 93, 110; ♿

Beer connoisseurs will welcome
the sight of the stainless-steel
tanks above the bar. Be merry with
tasty microbrews like the delicious
Honey Beer or the refreshing India
Pale Ale.

## Ⓨ CLÁSICA Y MODERNA
*Cafe, Bar*

☎ 4812-8707; www.clasicaymoderna
.com, in Spanish; Av Callao 892, Recoleta;
⏰ 8am-1am Mon-Wed, 8am-3am Fri &
Sat; Ⓜ Line D Callao; ♿

Mingle with an arty, intellectual
crowd at this good-looking 'multi-
espacio' (it's a cafe, bar, restaurant,
art space, bookstore and music
venue all rolled into one). Both
classic and modern – hence the
name – it fills to capacity for jazz
performances and poetry readings.

## Ⓨ LA BIELA *Cafe*

☎ 4804-0449; www.labiela.com; Av
Quintana 600, Recoleta; ⏰ 7am-late;
🚌 10, 17, 60, 92, 110; ♿

There's no need to squabble over
a few outdoor tables: La Biela's
huge patio, shaded by the leafy
branches of a formidable *gomero*
(rubber) tree, has enough sidewalk
seating for the entire national *fútbol* team (and their dear mothers,
too). Take a break from sightseeing
with coffee at this refined corner
institution just off Plaza Francia.

## Ⓨ MILIÓN *Bar*

☎ 4815-9925; www.milion.com.ar;
Paraná 1048, Barrio Norte; ⏰ noon-2am
Mon-Wed, noon-3am Thu, noon-4am
Fri, 8pm-late Sat & Sun; 🚌 10, 29, 39,
102, 152

True to its name, Milión looks like
a million dollars – the restored
mansion comprises a gorgeous
open-air courtyard brightened
by twinkle lights and a grand
outdoor staircase that leads to
the upper-level bar. Pretty young
things sprawling on the moonlit
steps, sipping frozen mojitos
and basil daiquiris, complete the
picture.

**Ral Veroni**

*Visual artist, printmaker & poet; co-owner of Galeria Mar Dulce*

**Describe your work.** I work with the old art of emblems. When I have money, I paint. When I have less money, I draw. When I have no money, I write. **You left Argentina for a while.** I went to the US as an artist-in-residence and to Europe as an MFA student. But I always remembered the unique energy of Buenos Aires. In comparison to Europe, Argentina doesn't have much state funding for the arts. It's part of the reason that public and alternative art forms have grown here. Our gallery isn't for profit – it's a romantic project. **Which Argentinian artists do you admire?** Jorge Pirozzi [who's exhibited at Papelera Palermo, p117], Bruno Dubner [who's exhibited at Palais de Glace, p95], Alfredo Benavinez Bedoya, Diego Bianchi. **Best places to see art?** Tourists like the modern feel of MALBA (p105) and Fundación Proa (p86), but I prefer Museo Nacional de Bellas Artes (p94) or Museo Xul Solar (p94).

# PLAY

## BASEMENT CLUB
*Dance Club*

☎ 4812-3584; www.theshamrockbar
.com; Rodríguez Peña 1220, Recoleta;
🕐 midnight-late, depending on event;
Ⓜ Line D Callao; 🚌 10, 21, 39, 101, 152

The Basement Club pulls in a jovial
mix of expats, locals and travelers
with house music and inexpensive
drinks. Hit the extended happy
hour at the popular Shamrock pub
upstairs before descending into
the subterranean club.

## GLAM *Gay Club*

☎ 4963-2521; www.glambsas.com
.ar; José Antonio Cabrera 3046, Barrio
Norte; 🕐 1am-late Thu-Sat; 🚌 29, 92,
109, 111

One of BA's hottest gay clubs,
Glam comprises three floors,
several bars and lounges, and a
sweaty dance floor that fills with
genetically blessed porteño males.
Come late (3am is ideal) for the
best scenery.

## NOTORIOUS *Jazz Club*

☎ 4813-6888, 4815-8473; www
.notorious.com.ar, in Spanish; Av Callao
966, Recoleta; 🕐 from 9pm; Ⓜ Line D
Callao; ♿

This intimate jazz venue attracts
all ages – devoted locals and curious travelers alike – with nightly
gigs of serious jazz and world
music. Book ahead and visit the
record shop before settling in for
a show.

# >PALERMO

Filled with open green spaces where fitness-crazed locals can run and play to their hearts' content, Palermo is a largely residential barrio that separates Recoleta from Palermo Viejo. The neighborhood crawls with stroller-pushing mothers and muscular men racing each other past the rose gardens of sprawling Parque 3 de Febrero (Palermo Woods), a leafy section that also contains the city's botanical gardens, zoo and Japanese gardens, all surrounded by modern high-rise apartment buildings. But there's more to this area than fresh air and middle class comforts. Palermo is home to several embassies and a wealth of museums, from the classic MALBA to the intriguing Evita Museum and the stately Museum of Decorative Arts. Quiet by night, the neighborhood's main thoroughfares, Av Santa Fe and Av del Libertador, buzz during the day with art students on their way to study famous paintings, teenagers typing text messages outside fancy shopping malls, and ambassadors meeting for coffee in elegant glass-fronted cafes.

# PALERMO

## 👁 SEE
Jardín Botánico
  Carlos Thays ..............1  A3
Jardín Japonés
  (entrance) ..................2  C2
Jardín Zoológico ........3  B3
La Rural .........................4  A2
MALBA (Museo de Arte
  Latinoamericano
  de Buenos Aires) .....5  D2
Monumento a los
  Españoles ................6  B2
Monumento a Sarmiento 7  B2
Museo de Arte Popular
  José Hernández ........8  C3
Museo de Artes Plásticas
  Eduardo Sívori ........9  A1

Museo Evita ..............10  B3
Museo Nacional de
  Arte Decorativo ......11  D3
Parque 3 de Febrero ....12  B1

## 🏠 SHOP
Alto Palermo ..............13  C5
Jeans Makers ..............14  A5
Paseo Alcorta ..............15  D2

## 🍴 EAT
Artemisia ....................16  A6
Museo Evita
  Restaurante ..........(see 10)
Tea Connection ..........17  C3

## ⭐ PLAY
Bulnes Class ..............18  B6
Club Aráoz ..................19  B4
Crobar ........................20  A1
La Peña del Colorado ...21  B4
Thelonious Club ..........22  B4

## ◉ SEE

### ◉ JARDÍN BOTÁNICO CARLOS THAYS

☎ 4831-4527; Av Santa Fe 3951, Palermo; admission free; ☀ 8am-8pm Nov-Mar & 9am-6pm Apr-Oct; Ⓜ Line D Plaza Italia; ♿

Escape the din of Plaza Italia inside this lush botanical garden, designed by renowned landscape architect Carlos Thays and opened in 1898. It blooms with over 3000 tree and plant species, Roman-style sculptures, floating lily pads on still ponds and an antique iron-and-glass greenhouse originally shown at the 1900 Paris Exhibition.

### ◉ JARDÍN JAPONÉS

☎ 4804-4922; www.jardinjapones.org. ar, in Spanish; cnr Avs Figueroa Alcorta & Casares, Palermo; admission $8; Mon-Fri $3, Sat & Sun $4; ☀ 10am-6pm; 🚌 10, 37, 67, 102, 130; ♿

Paper lanterns flutter in the breeze, enormous koi fish cluster at the water's edge, tourists snap photos from a footbridge – these are the Japanese gardens, a 1967 gift from the Japanese immigrant community to Buenos Aires. Rare flowers and artificial waterways set an exotic stage for frequent cultural events, yoga classes and tea ceremonies. Stop for sushi in the pagoda-style restaurant.

### ◉ JARDÍN ZOOLÓGICO

☎ 4011-9900; www.zoobuenosaires .com.ar; cnr Avs Las Heras & Sarmiento, Palermo; adult/under 12yr $18/free; ☀ 10am-6pm Tue-Sun; Ⓜ Line D Plaza Italia; ♿

What, you've never heard of a *vicuña*? Even eight-year-old por-teños (BA locals) are familiar with this super-skinny camel relative. Expand your knowledge of South American wildlife at the city zoo, which, while overdue for a renovation, houses a host of unusual indigenous animals and kids' favorites like kangaroos and polar bears. The zoo's structures – resembling temples, Roman ruins, and the like – mimic the architecture of the animals' native lands.

### LA RURAL

Fashion week, book fairs, farm shows and tango extravaganzas – since 1878, the city's biggest festivals and events have taken place at **La Rural** ( ☎ 4777-5500; www.larural.com.ar; Plaza Italia). The sprawling urban fairgrounds and convention center, dating to 1878 and conveniently located on Plaza Italia, comprise a series of auditoriums, pavilions and outdoor green spaces. The complex swarms with cattle and cowboys during July's La Rural, the venue's signature livestock show, while intellectual types and art collectors take over the place during annual events like arteBA (p24) and the Feria del Libro (p24).

adventurous temporary exhibits. It also fosters an active film preservation program with a regular schedule of art-house cinema. The design-minded museum shop and cafe are popular with Palermo's art lovers.

### ◎ MONUMENTO A LOS ESPAÑOLES

**cnr Avs del Libertador & Sarmiento, Palermo;** Ⓜ **Line D Plaza Italia;** 🚌 **10, 33, 34**

This magnificent white monument on broad Av del Libertador was built in 1927. The massive figures at its base represent four regions of Argentina: the Pampas, the Andes, the Chaco and Río de La Plata.

### ◎ MONUMENTO A SARMIENTO

**cnr Avs del Libertador & Sarmiento, Palermo;** Ⓜ **Line D Plaza Italia;** 🚌 **10, 33, 34**

Rodin crafted this statue of former Argentine president Domingo F Sarmiento, the country's leader from 1868 to 1874 and a key figure in Argentina's education system.

### ◎ MUSEO DE ARTE POPULAR JOSÉ HERNÁNDEZ

☎ **4803-2384; www.mujose.org.ar, in Spanish; Av del Libertador 2373; admission $1, Sun free;** 🕑 **1-7pm Wed-Fri, 10am-8pm Sat & Sun;** 🚌 **10, 37, 59, 60, 92**

This small but appealing museum has a permanent collection of

Animals of all sizes live at Jardín Zoológico

### ◎ MALBA (MUSEO DE ARTE LATINOAMERICANO DE BUENOS AIRES)

☎ **4808-6500; www.malba.org.ar, in Spanish; Av Figueroa Alcorta 3415, Palermo; admission $22, Wed $10;** 🕑 **noon-9pm Wed, noon-8pm Thu-Mon;** 🚌 **17, 67, 124, 130;** ♿

Opened in 2001, this landmark contemporary museum houses the Costantini collection of modern Latin American art, along with indigenous Argentine crafts and popular arts, including colorful textiles, decorative masks and Carnaval costumes.

### 🖸 MUSEO DE ARTES PLÁSTICAS EDUARDO SÍVORI

☎ 4774-9452; www.museosivori.org.ar, in Spanish; Parque 3 de Febrero, Av de la Infanta Isabel 555, Palermo; admission $1, free Wed & Sat; 🕙 noon-8pm Tue-Fri, 10am-8pm Sat & Sun, until 8pm Dec-Jun; 🚍 10, 34; ♿

Tucked into a quiet corner of Parque 3 de Febrero (Palermo Woods; opposite), this modern art museum shows an outstanding collection of paintings and sculptures by over 100 of Argentina's best artists.

### 🖸 MUSEO EVITA

☎ 4807-9433; www.museoevita.org; Lafinur 2988, Palermo; admission $15; 🕙 11am-7pm Tue-Sun; 🚍 15, 59, 60, 64, 93; Ⓜ Line D Plaza Italia ♿

Whether saint or tyrant (a question posed by the museum's first display), Evita is an icon. The museum dedicated to her life is located in an old building that the first lady's foundation once used as a women's shelter. Check out her glamorous outfits before dining in the courtyard restaurant (p109).

### 🖸 MUSEO NACIONAL DE ARTE DECORATIVO

☎ 4801-8248; www.mnad.org; Av del Libertador 1902, Palermo; admission $5, free Tue; 🕙 2-7pm Tue-Sun, closed Mon Jan-Feb; 🚍 21, 38, 59, 60, 118; ♿

Housed in an opulent beaux-arts mansion that once belonged to Chilean aristocrats, this museum displays some 4000 pieces of decorative art, from Louis XIV furniture to Renaissance paint-

### MAD FOR *MATE*

Starbucks may have infiltrated the city (the first branch of the megachain opened in 2008 in the Alto Palermo shopping center), but you won't see many locals toting styrofoam cups of coffee through the city streets. South Americans are long-time consumers of *mate*, a tea-like drink made by pouring hot water over the leaves of *yerba mate*, a native holly plant. Just as their north-of-the-equator counterparts have portable coffee mugs, Argentines use specific *mate* accoutrements: they pour hot water from a large thermos into a spherical gourd filled with *mate* leaves, then sip the drink through a metal *bombilla* (straw). And porteños drink a *lot* of it – you'll see locals of all ages and economic classes carrying *mate* cases and sipping from gourds at the office, on the street, on picnic blankets and rooftop terraces. *Mate* is an acquired taste, but don't miss the chance to taste it when someone offers – passing around the gourd with friends is a fundamental social ritual.

There are plenty of outdoor activities at Parque 3 de Febrero

ings. The outdoor cafe in the front courtyard is a perfectly quaint setting for a glass of wine.

###  PARQUE 3 DE FEBRERO
**cnr Avs del Libertador & de la Infanta Isabel, Palermo;** 🚌 **10, 34, 130;** ♿
Also known as Bosques de Palermo, or Palermo Woods, this sweeping green space abounds with small lakes and paddleboats, pretty gazeboes, stands renting bikes and in-line skates, a monument to literary greats called El Jardín de las Poetas (the Garden of Poets), and the exquisite Rosedal (rose garden).

Watch your step at night, when Av de la Infanta Isabel becomes a transvestite red-light zone.

## 🛍 SHOP
### 🏬 ALTO PALERMO
*Shopping Mall*
☎ **5777-8000; www.altopalermo.com .ar, in Spanish; Av Coronel Díaz 2098, Palermo;** 🕐 **10am-10pm;** Ⓜ **Line D Bulnes**
Smack on stylish Av Santa Fe, this shiny mall specializes in chic clothing boutiques, jewelry stores, home-decor emporiums – and the city's first Starbucks.

## ABASTO & ONCE

The bustling barrios of Abasto and Once, while a little dodgy at night, are part of the 'real' Buenos Aires that's largely unaffected by the tourist trade. Walk west from Congreso along Av Corrientes, or take a quick taxi or Subte ride, to reach this cultural melting pot and commercial district crammed with colorful fabric shops and family-run Jewish and Peruvian eateries. The neighborhood's centerpiece is the historic Mercado de Abasto, previously a massive fresh produce market and now a beautifully restored structure that houses the shopping mall called simply **El Abasto** ( ☎ 4959-3400; www.abasto-shopping.com.ar, in Spanish; cnr Avs Corrientes & Anchorena; ⏰ 10am-10pm; Ⓜ Line B Carlos Gardel). Nearby, on a gentrified street off Av Anchorena is the former home of tango legend Carlos Gardel – now the small but fascinating **Museo Casa Carlos Gardel** ( ☎ 4964-2071; www.museocasacarlosgardel.buenosaires.gob.ar; Jean Jaurés 735; admission $1, free Wed; ⏰ 10am-7pm Sat & Sun; Ⓜ Line B Carlos Gardel). The small tasting cellar at **0800-Vino** ( ☎ 0800-VINO; www.0800-vino.com, in Spanish; Av Anchorena 695; Ⓜ Line B Carlos Gardel; see also p16) is just a stone's throw from the tango legend's homestead, and one of the city's premiere alternative theater spaces and cultural centers, the bohemian **Ciudad Cultural Konex** ( ☎ 4864-3200; www.ciudadculturalkonex.org, in Spanish; Av Sarmiento 3131; Ⓜ Line B Carlos Gardel), is housed in a renovated factory a few blocks away.

### 🔲 JEANS MAKERS
*Fashion*

☎ 4865-2420; www.jeansmakers.com; Soler 4202, Palermo; ⏰ 11am-9pm Mon-Sat; 🚌 39, 92, 152

Your prayers have been answered. As the name suggests, Jeans Makers lets you custom-design your own denims. Get your style down to a science by combining the flattering cut of your favorite pair with cool stitching options and a range of design detail choices – and voilà! You've got the jeans of your dreams.

### 🔲 PASEO ALCORTA
*Shopping Mall*

☎ 5777-6500; www.paseoalcorta .com.ar; Salguero 3172, Palermo Chico; ⏰ 10am-10pm

This upmarket shopping mall showcases stylish Argentine brands, exclusive European designers, a ritzy food court, a cinema center and a children's play area.

## 🍴 EAT

### 🔲 ARTEMISIA *Vegetarian* $$

☎ 4863-4242; www.artemisiaresto .com.ar; José Antonio Cabrera 3877, Palermo; ⏰ 8:30pm-late Tue-Sat; 🚌 36, 92, 106; Ⓥ

The homey, vegetarian-friendly Artemisia is ideal for a low-key dinner of freshly baked brown bread, inventive tapas like zucchini bruschetta and mini caprese skewers, and heart-healthy wok dishes.

### 🔲 MUSEO EVITA RESTAURANTE
*Modern Argentine* $$

☎ 4800-1599; www.museoevita.org; JM Gutierrez 3926, Palermo; ⏰ 9am-midnight; Ⓜ Line D Plaza Italia; ♿ Ⓥ ♿

Fear not, tourists – though this eatery is located at the Evita museum (p106), it's not a thematic restaurant. The charming tiled courtyard is in fact a picture-perfect spot for lunch, and the cuisine is thoroughly sophisticated. Refined waiters

### SWEET TREATS

With so many foodies analyzing Argentina's beef and waxing poetic about the wine, it's easy to overlook one of the city's finest epicurean delights – *helado* (ice cream). Thanks to Argentina's Italian immigrants, most of the ice cream in Buenos Aires is delightfully rich and available in exotic flavors from *dulce de leche* (a caramel-like local treat) to *maracuya* (passion fruit). *Heladerías* (ice-cream parlors) offer free samples of their creamy concoctions before you commit to a flavor (or three). Satiate your sweet tooth properly at a shop displaying the words *elaboración artesanal* – this is the real deal, handmade on the premises – or one of the larger *helado* franchises around the city.

Taking a rest from the life of Eva Perón at Museo Evita Restaurante

deliver gourmet risotto, pizza and steak to alfresco diners. The first lady's biggest fans prefer to dine inside amid the Evita memorabilia.

### 🍴 TEA CONNECTION
*Cafe, International*     $$
☎ 4807-5034; www.teaconnection.com.ar; Cerviño 3550, Palermo; ⏱ 8am-midnight Mon-Sat, from 9am Sun; 🚌 37, 59, 60, 92, 93
At this sleek eatery and cafe, choose from health-conscious sandwiches, fresh salads and vegetable tarts, plus over 30 types of black, red and green teas. Try the fantastic fruit-infused water – the *maracuyá* blend evokes a Brazilian beach.

## ⭐ PLAY
### ⭐ BULNES CLASS *Gay Bar*
☎ 4861-7492; www.bulnesclass.com.ar, in Spanish; Bulnes 1250, Palermo;

⏱ 11pm-late Fri & Sat; 🚌 26, 92, 106, 128; ♿
Bulnes Class attracts a mostly gay crowd to its stylish, minimalist bar. Drop in after dinner but before hitting a club.

### ⭐ CLUB ARÁOZ *Dance Club*
☎ 4832-9751; www.clubaraoz.com.ar, in Spanish; Aráoz 2424, Palermo; ⏱ 1am-late Fri & Sat; 🚌 36, 39, 106, 152
Homesick for hip-hop? Sidestep the city's electrónica scene and head to Club Aráoz to see local break-dancers doing their thing, disco kids throwing back Fernet-and-Coca-Cola cocktails, and music videos illuminating the big screen.

### ⭐ CROBAR *Dance Club*
☎ 4778-1500; www.crobar.com.ar; Marcelo Freyre s/n, Palermo; ⏱ 10pm-late Fri & Sat; 🚌 10, 34, 36

## I'VE GOT RESERVATIONS

No one wants to spend precious hours of their vacation waiting in a long queue of hungry, hopeful restaurant patrons. Make sure you're not lost in the dinner crowd by following a few guidelines.

> **Lunch early.** Porteños lunch later, so go at noon to snag a table.
> **Book on weekends.** Reserve ahead of time – and confirm it – on chaotic Friday and Saturday nights.
> **Dinner?** Go early or go late. An empty restaurant isn't appealing, but venues like Gran Bar Danzon (p98) have cocktail bars that draw an earlier crowd. If you don't mind dining late, have a glass of wine at the bar and wait for the night's first sitting to clear out.
> **If you can't book, have a backup plan.** If your heart's set on one restaurant, make sure it's in an area with options – if you can't get in, you'll discover something good (and less hyped) just around the corner.

Nothing beats strong drinks and a supremely attractive crowd of local twenty- and thirty-somethings writhing around on the dance floor. Don't dress to the nines at Crobar – the atmosphere is trendy, but in a laid-back way – and come late on a Friday night for the best scene.

### ☆ LA PEÑA DEL COLORADO
*Folk Music*
☎ 4822-1038; www.delcolorado.com.ar;
**Güemes 3657, Palermo; admission $25;**
🕑 8pm-late; Ⓜ Line D Bulnes; ♿
This lively spot – which many porteños swear is the best *peña* (folk music venue) in the city – puts on live *folklórica* shows. After the musical set, the performers pass around guitars and country-style

instruments so the happy-go-lucky crowd can get in on the singing and strumming action. Diners can order a set menu ($50) or from the a la carte menu. See also p19.

### ☆ THELONIOUS CLUB
*Jazz Club*
☎ 4829-1562; www.theloniousclub
.com.ar; Salguero 1884, Palermo; admission $10-15; 🕑 9pm-late Wed-Sun;
Ⓜ Line D Bulnes; ♿
Get into the jazz mood with a bourbon-infused 'smoky martini' at the bar – or share a bottle of wine in a cozy, darkened booth. The slick, intimate music club features a dynamic agenda of superb live jazz.

# >PALERMO VIEJO

Any porteña (BA local) worth her leather clutch purse will tell you that Palermo Viejo is the city's most fashion-forward neighborhood. The heart of the local design and dining scenes bustles by day with stylish young women lugging shopping bags around the designer markets on Plaza Serrano and hipsters clicking through their MacBooks in New York–style delis. By night, the leafy streets throng with beautiful people and serious foodies en route to one of the neighborhood's countless chic eateries and cocktail bars. In case there was any question, the names of Palermo Viejo's subdivisions, Palermo Soho (around Plaza Serrano) and Palermo Hollywood (the hub of BA's film industry, located just across the railroad tracks), clearly reveal the cosmopolitan aspirations of the barrio's trendsetting denizens. This part of town is short on formal sightseeing attractions, but a simple stroll through Palermo Viejo – and its busy designer fairs, petite cobblestoned plazas, low-rise colonial buildings, posh boutiques and sidewalk cafes swarming with voguish locals – provides plenty of cultural stimulation.

## PALERMO VIEJO

### 🛍 SHOP

| | | |
|---|---|---|
| 28 Sport | 1 | E4 |
| Calma Chicha | 2 | E4 |
| Cora Groppo | 3 | E4 |
| Corre Lola | 4 | E5 |
| DAM | 5 | E4 |
| Felix | 6 | E4 |
| Hermanos Estebecorena | 7 | B1 |
| Humawaca | 8 | E4 |
| Juana de Arco | 9 | E4 |
| Lo de Joaquin Alberdi | 10 | E3 |
| Nadine Zlotogora | 11 | E4 |
| Papelera Palermo | 12 | E4 |
| Rapsodia | 13 | E4 |

### 🍴 EAT

| | | |
|---|---|---|
| Azema Exotic Bistró | 14 | C2 |
| Bio | 15 | D2 |

| | | |
|---|---|---|
| Bo Bo | 16 | F3 |
| Cluny | 17 | F4 |
| Don Julio | 18 | F3 |
| Freud y Fahler | 19 | E4 |
| Green Bamboo | 20 | C1 |
| Il Ballo di Mattone | 21 | C2 |
| La Dorita | 22 | D2 |
| La Fábrica del Taco | 23 | D4 |
| Little Rose | 24 | E4 |
| Miranda | 25 | C2 |
| Ølsen | 26 | B2 |
| Sarkis | 27 | C5 |
| Social Paraíso | 28 | D4 |
| Sudestada | 29 | D1 |

### 🍸 DRINK

| | | |
|---|---|---|
| Bangalore Pub & Curry House | 30 | C3 |
| Bar 6 | 31 | E4 |
| Caracas | 32 | F3 |

| | | |
|---|---|---|
| Carnal | 33 | C3 |
| Casa Cruz | 34 | D3 |
| Home Hotel | 35 | B2 |
| Lelé de Troya | 36 | E3 |
| Malas Artes | 37 | E4 |
| Mark's Deli | 38 | E4 |
| Mundo Bizarro | 39 | D5 |
| Oui Oui | 40 | C1 |
| Sugar | 41 | E3 |

### ⭐ PLAY

| | | |
|---|---|---|
| Bach Bar | 42 | F5 |
| La Viruta | 43 | D5 |
| Los Cardones | 44 | F3 |
| Niceto Club | 45 | B3 |
| Salon Canning | 46 | E5 |
| Sitges | 47 | F6 |

Please see over for map

#  SHOP

## 📷 28 SPORT
*Shoes*

☎ 4831-4287; www.28sport.com; Gurruchaga 1481, Palermo Viejo; ⏰ 11am-1:30pm & 2:30-8pm Mon-Sat; 🚌 93, 142

These funky, two-tone sneakers and boots are affordable and beautifully made with high-quality Argentine leather. The retro shop channels 1950s Americana.

## 📷 CALMA CHICHA
*Fashion, Home Decor*

☎ 4831-1818; www.calmachicha .com; Gurruchaga 1580, Palermo Viejo; ⏰ 10am-8pm Mon-Sat, noon-8pm Sun; 🚌 15, 55, 57, 140, 151, 168

The fun, well-priced accessories and home decor at Calma Chicha use Argentine materials to produce items ranging from practical – leather messenger bags and placemats – to kitschy objects like patchwork cowhide throw rugs. A second location is at Honduras 4925.

## 📷 CORA GROPPO
*Women's Fashion*

☎ 4833-7474; www.coragroppo.com; cnr El Salvador & Armenia, Palermo Viejo; ⏰ 11am-8pm Mon-Sat; 🚌 15, 39, 55, 168

The talked-about designer behind this sleek high-fashion line is legendary for her reworking of volume and texture in everyday garments. Cora Groppo's striking cropped jackets and multilayered wrap tops make a sophisticated

Stylish accessories (and cowhide throw rugs) abound at Calma Chicha

design statement without over-whelming an ensemble.

### 🖾 CORRE LOLA Shoes

☎ 4773-1335; www.correlola.com.ar, in Spanish; Niceto Vega 4691, Palermo Viejo; ⌚ 11am-1pm & 2-8pm Mon-Sat; 🚌 39, 152, 168

This whimsical footwear line (the name of which is a wink to the cult classic film *Run Lola Run*) fea-tures pretty ballerina flats in every color of the rainbow, knee-high boots in patent leather or rub-ber, cork wedge platforms with oversized flower appliqués and leather sandals in candy shades of jade and magenta.

### 🖾 DAM Women's Fashion

☎ 4833-3935; www.damboutique .com.ar; Honduras 4775, Palermo Viejo; ⌚ 11:30am-8:30pm Mon-Sat; 🚌 39, 55, 168

Spice up a boring black wardrobe with a brightly flowered 60s-style dress or a one-piece jumpsuit patterned with little green apples from DAM. Playful, vibrant, oc-casionally outrageous, designer Carola Besasso's casual line is a hit with artistic young porteñas.

### 🖾 FELIX
*Men's Fashion*

☎ 4832-2994; www.felixba.com .ar; Gurruchaga 1670, Palermo Viejo; ⌚ 11am-8pm Mon-Sat, 3-8pm Sun; 🚌 15, 39, 55

The spacious, brick-walled Felix stocks casual clothes for fashion-minded college kids and trendy men. You'll see these graphic T-shirts, trench coats, faded jeans, velvet sport jackets, tartan cotton shirts and vintage-inspired sneak-ers on boys out and about in the barrio.

## BUENOS AIRES BY BICYCLE

Thanks to aggressive motorists, cobblestones, thieves, pollution, speeding *colectivos* (buses) and meat-delivery trucks serving as impromptu roadblocks, hitting the streets of Buenos Aires on a bike is not for the faint of heart. But like many other international capitals, the city has become considerably more cyclist-friendly in the past two years. A new system of protected bike paths provides a safe passage along several transporta-tion arteries. A community bike-lending program, **Mejor en Bici** (www.mejorenbici. gob.ar), recently opened bicycle-sharing stations to the porteño public (Buenos Aires locals; tourists with proof of an address in Buenos Aires are also eligible to participate). The best way to see the city on two wheels is to rent a bicycle or book a tour through La Bicicleta Naranja (p168) or Urban Biking (p168) or to join the **Masa Critica** (www. masacriticabsas.com.ar) city-wide cycle at 4pm on the first Sunday of the month — meet at the Obelisk.

## 🏠 HERMANOS ESTEBECORENA
*Men's Fashion*

☎ 4772-2145; www.hermanosestebe
corena.com; El Salvador 5960, Palermo
Hollywood; ⏱ 11am-1pm & 1:30-9pm
Mon-Fri, 11am-9pm Sat; 🚌 39, 93, 111
Male urbanites seeking stylish,
understated cool have found their
mecca at Hermanos Estebecorena.
Exquisite tailoring, unusual text-
ures and sleek cuts characterize
this smart line of slim-cut corduroy
trousers, reversible bomber
jackets and dapper raincoats.

## 🏠 HUMAWACA *Leather*

☎ 4832-2662; www.humawaca.com; El
Salvador 4692, Palermo Viejo; ⏱ 11am-
8pm Mon-Sat, 2-7pm Sun; 🚌 34, 55, 166
Award-winning designer Ingrid
Gutman brings both form and
functionality to Argentine leather,
producing handbags, backpacks
and wallets with clean modernist
lines. You'll also see her distinctive
collection for sale at MALBA (p105).

## 🏠 JUANA DE ARCO
*Women's Fashion*

☎ 4833-1621; www.juanadearco.net; El
Salvador 4762, Palermo Viejo; ⏱ 11am-
8pm Mon-Sat, 2-8pm Sun; 🚌 34, 39,
55, 166
Designer Mariana Cortés, beloved
for her whimsical approach to
casual women's fashion, is
the creative force behind this
exuberant collection of patterned

underwear, crocheted swimsuits,
conversation-starting woven
accessories and animal-stamped
pillow cases.

## 🏠 LO DE JOAQUIN ALBERDI
*Wine*

☎ 4832-5329; www.lodejoaquinalberdi
.com.ar; Jorge Luis Borges 1772, Palermo
Viejo; ⏱ noon-9:30pm; 🚌 34, 39, 55, 168
Argentine wines for every taste
and budget line the racks and
cellar of this attractive wine shop.
Pop across the street to the sister
wine-bar, Cabernet, for a glass of
Malbec on the patio.

## 🏠 NADINE ZLOTOGORA
*Fashion*

☎ 4831-4203; www.nadinez.com; El
Salvador 4638, Palermo Viejo; ⏱ 11am-
8pm Mon-Sat; 🚌 15, 39, 55
The quirky, feminine fashions of
Nadine Zlotogora exude old-world
romance and rustic charm. Recent
collections have featured delicate
lace and crushed velvet, fitted bod-
ices, long jackets and multilayered
skirts. The men's line includes patterned coats and unconventional
takes on classic trousers and shirts.

## 🏠 PAPELERA PALERMO
*Paper, Gifts*

☎ 4833-3081; www.papelerapalermo
.com.ar, in Spanish; Honduras 4945,
Palermo Viejo; ⏱ 10am-8pm Mon-Sat,
2-8pm Sun; 🚌 15, 39, 55, 168

This fashionable paper store is a dream come true for aesthetically minded writers. Stock up on handmade stationery, journals, stamped wrapping paper, stylish address books and beautiful postcards. Cowhide notebooks and tongue-in-cheek Evita photo albums also make unorthodox vacation mementos.

### 🏠 RAPSODIA
*Women's Fashion*

☎ 4832-5363; www.rapsodia.com.ar, in Spanish; El Salvador 4757, Palermo Viejo; 🕙 10am-8pm Mon-Sat, noon-9pm Sun; 🚌 15, 57, 110, 141, 160

According to Rapsodia's designers, this bohemian clothing line was created for women who love music, art and travel. Stop by for flirty skirts, flowing '70s-influenced sundresses and lived-in jeans.

## 🍴 EAT

### 🍴 AZEMA EXOTIC BISTRÓ
*French, International*                  $$$

☎ 4774-4191; Angel Justiniano Carranza 1875, Palermo Hollywood; 🕙 8pm-late Mon-Sat; 🚌 39, 93, 111, 161; 🚻 Ⓥ

With exotic spices and foreign ingredients, Paul Jean Azema bravely goes where few local chefs have gone before. His eclectic eatery takes inspiration from his diverse travels – tandoori salmon, Vietnamese noodles and tangy ceviche all have their place on the menu – and the simple French-style space is inviting.

### 🍴 BIO *Vegetarian*               $$

☎ 4774-3880; www.biorestaurant.com.ar, in Spanish; cnr Humboldt & Guatemala, Palermo Hollywood; 🕙 noon-late; 🚌 9, 11, 93; Ⓥ 🚻

### CLOSED-DOOR DINING

There's no shortage of fine-dining venues in Palermo Viejo, but as local foodies often moan, overpopulated dining rooms and aloof wait staff can detract from the gastronomic experience. For a refreshing alternative, check out the much-talked-about *puerta cerrada* (closed door) scene. These intimate eateries, often run out of the chef's home, host just a handful of guests. Fresh seasonal dishes are served in a dinner-party-like atmosphere at **Casa Felix** (www.diegofelix.com). At new-on-the-scene **Cocina Garden** (http://cocinagarden.blogspot.com), guests dine on American-inspired cuisine on a romantic candlelit patio. At **Cocina Sunae** (www.cocinasunae.com), chef Christina Sunae Wiseman adds a contemporary twist to traditional Korean, Vietnamese and Thai recipes handed down from her grandmother. If communal dining isn't your thing, try the northern Argentine cuisine in the courtyard at **Almacén Secreto** (www.almacensecretoclub.blogspot.com) or the gourmet tasting menu at **Treintasillas** (www.treintasillas.com). In true 'underground' style, addresses are provided when you reserve.

Sneak a peek at the kitchen at Scandinavian restaurant Ølsen (p121)

So your better half's a devoted carnivore but you're dying for green cuisine? Don't drag them kicking and screaming to an extreme organic eatery, just take them to Bio for fantastically fresh pastas and salads. The homemade ginger lemonade is heavenly.

### 🍴 BO BO
*Modern Argentine* $$
☎ 4774-0505; www.bobohotel.com; Guatemala 4882, Palermo Soho; 🕒 8am-late Mon-Sat, to 5pm Sun; Ⓜ Line D Plaza Italia
Located inside one of the city's original (and best) boutique hotels, Bo Bo does gourmet Mediterranean dishes with a local

twist. Foodies go for the five-course tasting menu with wine pairings, while budget-conscious travelers show up for the prix-fixe lunch.

### 🍴 CLUNY
*Modern European, Argentine* $$$
☎ 4831-7176; El Salvador 4618, Palermo Viejo; 🕒 noon-late Mon-Sat; 🚌 15, 39, 55, 160; ♿
Warm, elegant and stylish, Cluny is a class act. The French-inflected dishes, including duck magret, beef with mustard sauce (divine) and Patagonian lamb with couscous, are beautifully prepared and keep the well-heeled locals coming back.

## 🍴 DON JULIO *Parrilla*   $$

☎ 4831-9564; Cnr Guatemala & Gurruchaga, Palermo Viejo; ⏱ noon-4pm & 8pm-midnight; 🚌 39, 93, 111; ♿ 👶

Classy service and fine wines add an upscale bent to this traditional corner steakhouse. Of course, the *bife de chorizo* (sirloin) is the main attraction at Don Julio, but the exposed-brick interior, dark-wood cutting boards and leather placemats enhance the sensory experience, and the gourmet salads – served with a flourish by the uber-professional wait staff – are a treat.

## 🍴 FREUD Y FAHLER
*Modern Argentine*   $$

☎ 4833-2153; Gurruchaga 1750, Palermo Viejo; ⏱ noon-3:30pm & 8pm-midnight Mon-Sat; 🚌 39, 55; Ⓥ

Freud y Fahler, despite the name, isn't a high-concept eatery – the cozy, upscale corner spot offers a simple menu of gourmet Mediterranean-inspired and modern Argentine steaks, pastas, risottos and salads. The art gallery crowd often fills the petite space at lunchtime.

## 🍴 GREEN BAMBOO
*Vietnamese*   $$$

☎ 4775-7050; www.green-bamboo .com.ar, in Spanish; cnr Costa Rica & Angel Justiniana Carranza, Palermo Hollywood; ⏱ 8.30pm-late; 🚌 39, 93, 111, 161; Ⓥ

Retro-Asian and kitschy cool, Green Bamboo is paradise for those craving flavorful Vietnamese cuisine. Reserve ahead – this darkened corner space always gets busy – and start with a signature cocktail made with mint, papaya or passion fruit. Then park yourself in a cushioned corner booth for tongue-searing soups, nutty noodle dishes and savory pork dishes.

## 🍴 IL BALLO DEL MATTONE
*Italian*   $$

☎ 4776-4247; www.ilballo.tv; Gorriti 5737, Palermo Hollywood; ⏱ noon-late; 🚌 39, 93, 111

This pint-sized trattoria is the flagship location of a Little Italy empire that's recently popped up. Squeeze in (you'll need reservations) and order from the chalkboard menu of homemade pasta and red wine.

## 🍴 LA DORITA *Parrilla*   $$

☎ 4773-0070; cnr Humboldt & Costa Rica, Palermo Hollywood; ⏱ noon-4pm & 8pm-1am; 🚌 21, 111, 161; 👶

Back-to-basics La Dorita grills up well-priced steaks served in a casual atmosphere – televised *fútbol* games indoors, sidewalk tables outdoors. The *parrilla* (grill restaurant) is so popular with locals that it's grown a bigger sibling, La Dorita Enfrente, on the same intersection. Order the house wine and a mini *parrillada* (mixed grill) of three different cuts of beef.

## 🍴 LA FÁBRICA DEL TACO
*Mexican*      $

☎ 4833-3534; www.lafabricadel taco.com; Gorriti 5062, Palermo Viejo; ⏱ 1pm-late Tue-Sun; 🚌 39, 55, 168

Savory *tacos al pastor* (pork tacos), strong margaritas, a quirky-cool interior – and a handy location a stone's throw from Plaza Serrano – made this new-on-the-scene Mexican joint popular from the get-go.

## 🍴 LITTLE ROSE
*Japanese*      $$

☎ 4833-9496; Armenia 1672, Palermo Viejo; ⏱ 12:30-4pm & 8:30pm-12:30am Mon-Sat; 🚌 39, 55, 93

Sashimi and sake are Little Rose's mainstays, but this is no minimalist sushi bar – the sultry candlelit interior is filled with mirrors, shadowy corners and dreamy photographs. Step off the busy shopping street and into this otherworldly little restaurant for a romantic dinner date.

## 🍴 MIRANDA *Parrilla*    $$

☎ 4771-4255; www.parrillamiranda. com; cnr Costa Rica & Fitz Roy, Palermo

Hollywood; ⏱ 9am-late; 🚌 39, 111, 161

Fashionable Miranda is the *parrilla* of choice for the breed of porteños who crave the classic grilled steaks and *chorizos* they grew up with, but who won't sacrifice style for red meat any day of the week.

## 🍴 ØLSEN *Scandinavian*   $$$

☎ 4776-7677; Gorriti 5870, Palermo Viejo; ⏱ noon-1:30am Tue-Sat, 10:30am-8pm Sun; 🚌 39, 93, 111, 161; ♿ V

With its hip, relaxed vibe, too-cool crowd and dramatic central fireplace, Ølsen could indeed be located in the frosty climes of Scandinavia. The cuisine and service are hit-and-miss, but the vodka selection is superlative. Luxuriate in the garden with a frozen red-berry cocktail – it looks straight out of a magazine – or come for the popular Sunday brunch.

## 🍴 SARKIS *Middle Eastern*   $

☎ 4772-4911; Thames 1101, Villa Crespo; ⏱ noon-3pm & 8pm-1am; 🚌 39, 55, 168

This popular spot is packed every night with groups of friends sharing delicious Middle Eastern dishes. Try *baquerones* (marinated sardines) and *parras rellenas* (stuffed grape leaves) or stick to classics like hummus, kebabs, couscous and lamb.

## COSTANERA NORTE

Dedicated clubbers know Buenos Aires is firmly positioned on the global clubbing map and will want to hit the clubs along the river on Costanera Norte, a 10-minute taxi ride from Palermo. Most clubs only open on Fridays and Saturdays from around 1am, don't get going until 3am, and don't close until 9am, so take your sunglasses. The best are **Pachá** (www.pacha buenosaires.com; Av Costanera Rafael Obligado), BA's oldest and best superclub boasting big-name DJs and a riverside terrace; **Mandarine** (www.mandarineclub.com; Av Sarmiento & Av Costanera Norte), big on Friday nights for progressive house with lounges on a waterfront terrace; **Jet** (www.jet-lounge.com.ar; Av Costanera Rafael Obligado), a superslick club offering more mainstream sounds; and **Caix** (www.caix-ba.com.ar; Salguero & Av Costanera Norte), which starts to heat up around 9am Sunday morning! During summer most clubs move to fashionable Punta del Este, Uruguay.

### 🍴 SOCIAL PARAÍSO
*Modern Argentine*  $$

☎ 4831-4556; www.socialparaiso
.com.ar, in Spanish; Honduras 5182,
Palermo Hollywood; ⏲ 12:30-3:30pm
& 8.30pm-midnight Tue-Sat, 12:30-4pm
Sun; 🚌 39, 55

One of the originals of the Palermo dining revolution, Social Paraíso is an understated bistro with a short, sophisticated menu that crosses exotic international ingredients with local gastronomic staples like steak, fish and Patagonian lamb.

### 🍴 SUDESTADA
*Southeast Asian*  $$$

☎ 4776-3777; www.sudestadabuenos
aires.com; cnr Guatemala & Fitz Roy,
Palermo Hollywood; ⏲ noon-3:30pm
& 8pm-midnight Mon-Sat; 🚌 15, 39,
55, 93

This minimalist corner space isn't what you'd expect of a Southeast Asian eatery, but Sudestada's curries are the real thing – fiery and flavorful, they'll have you flagging down a waiter for more *agua* in no time. It offers a welcome change from steak and potatoes.

## 🍸 DRINK

### 🍸 BANGALORE PUB & CURRY HOUSE *Bar, Pub*

☎ 4779-2621; Humboldt 1416, Palermo
Viejo; ⏲ 6pm-4am; 🚌 39, 152, 168

The spicy Indian sampler platters and juicy burgers at this English-style pub are just as good as the killer pitchers of gin & tonic. Keep company with a nightly horde of youthful locals and expats at Bangalore, run by the same masterminds behind San Telmo's Gibraltar (p80).

### BAR 6 *Bar, Cafe*

☎ 4833-6807; www.barseis.com, in Spanish; Armenia 1676, Palermo Viejo; 8am-late Mon-Sat; 🚌 15, 39, 160; ♿ 🚼

A stylish neighborhood classic, Bar 6 is open all day – you can drop by for eggs and coffee in the morning or show up at night to lounge on a red velvet couch with a bellini or a beer. The contemporary design, soaring ceilings and foxy crowd make up for the indifferent service.

### CARACAS *Bar*

☎ 4776-8704; www.caracasbar.com; Guatemala 4802, Palermo Viejo; 7:30pm-5am Mon-Fri, from 8:30pm Sat; 🚌 39, 55, 160

A welcome addition to Palermo's nightlife scene is this artistic bar and art space complete with a gorgeous open-air terrace, funky murals splashed across the walls, a rotating schedule of well-known DJs, and a short menu of Venezuelan-inspired dishes. Happy hour runs from 7:30pm to 11pm; as the night wears on, Caracas brings in the porteño hipster crowd.

### CARNAL *Bar*

☎ 4772-7582; Niceto Vega 5511, Palermo Viejo; 9pm-late Tue-Sat; 🚌 39, 152, 168

See and be seen – preferably in the open air with an icy vodka tonic in hand – on the rooftop terrace at Carnal. A great-looking local crowd shows up every weekend to this ever-popular watering hole.

### CASA CRUZ *Bar*

☎ 4833-1112; www.casacruz-restaurant.com; Uriarte 1658, Palermo Viejo; 8:30pm-late Mon-Sat; 🚌 34, 55, 166; ♿

This low-lit, drop-dead-gorgeous restaurant is perhaps better known for its happening cocktail bar than for its cuisine (which can be hit-and-miss). Lounge on the lobby's velvet sofas, mojito in hand, to observe a glamorous parade of actresses, athletes and investment bankers entering Casa Cruz through the massive bronze doorway.

### HOME HOTEL *Bar*

☎ 4778-1008; www.homebuenosaires.com; Honduras 5860, Palermo Viejo;

Sit on the summer terrace at Lelé de Troya (p124)

NEIGHBORHOODS

PALERMO VIEJO

⏰ 9:30am-11:30pm; 🚌 39, 93, 111; ♿ Ⓥ 🚻

This chic, laid-back bar is located inside Home, widely considered the city's coolest and most design-conscious boutique hotel (p136). On warm weekend evenings, DJs spin tunes on the petite poolside patio and the smartly dressed bar staff mix creative drinks.

### 🍸 LELÉ DE TROYA *Bar*

☎ 4832-2726; www.leledetroya.com; cnr Costa Rica & Thames, Palermo Viejo; ⏰ noon-late; 🚌 34, 39, 55, 168

Laid-back; boasts a summer terrace that's ideal for kicking back with a glass of white on a warm day.

### 🍸 MALAS ARTES
*Cafe, Bar*

☎ 4831-0743; cnr Honduras & Jorge Luis Borges, Palermo Viejo; ⏰ 8am-late; 🚌 34, 39, 55, 168; 🚻

This bohemian corner bar on Plaza Serrano has high ceilings, big picture windows and happy hour specials on beer and cocktails. The sidewalk tables are highly sought after on sunny days.

### 🍸 MARK'S DELI *Cafe*

☎ 4832-6244; www.markspalermo.com; cnr El Salvador & Armenia, Palermo Viejo; ⏰ 8:30am-9:30pm Mon-Sat, 10:30am-9pm Sun; 🚌 15, 39, 55; ♿ 🚻

Cool porteños and bagel-craving travelers pretend like they're in

New York at highbrow Mark's Deli, a Manhattan-style cafe that's nearly always packed. If you can score a table, the place is great for cappuccino-and-chocolate-chip cookies while you conduct a post-mortem on your shopping day.

### 🍸 MUNDO BIZARRO *Bar*

☎ 4773-1967; www.mundobizarrobar .com; Serrano 1222, Palermo Viejo; ⏰ 8pm-3am Sun-Wed, 8pm-4am Thu, 8pm-5am Fri & Sat; 🚌 34, 39, 55, 168

With its vibrant red walls and retro 1950s American diner vibe, Mundo Bizarro has been a Palermo institution for a decade. This cozy late-night bar draws names from the local music scene and film industry.

### 🍸 OUI OUI *Cafe*

☎ 4778-9614; www.ouioui.com.ar; Nicaragua 6068, Palermo Viejo; ⏰ 8am-8pm Tue-Fri; 🚌 39, 67, 152; 🚻

*Pain au chocolat* and shabby chic, anyone? Yes please. This immensely popular French-style cafe produces the goods – dark coffee, buttery croissants, jars of tangy lemonade – and boasts a cozy rose-colored interior that's just as charming. Come early to beat the porteña parade.

### 🍸 SUGAR *Bar*

☎ 4831-3276; www.sugarbuenosaires. com; Costa Rica 4619, Palermo Viejo; ⏰ noon-1am; 🚌 55, 111, 161

Savor French-style coffee and other delights at Oui Oui

This lively expat watering hole brings in a rowdy crowd with bargain-priced drink specials, comfort food for the homesick and shindigs revolving around political and athletic events – any excuse for a party.

 ## PLAY

### ☆ BACH BAR
*Lesbian Club*

☎ 15-5184-0137; www.bach-bar.com.ar, in Spanish; José Antonio Cabrera 4390, Palermo; ⏲ 11pm-late Wed-Sun; 🚌 39, 106, 109, 140, 168

This popular lesbian club hosts karaoke nights and raucous live drag shows on weekends.

### ☆ LA VIRUTA *Tango*
☎ 4774-6357; www.lavirutatango.com; Armenia 1366, Palermo Viejo; ⏲ class times vary, *milonga* midnight Fri-Sun; 🚌 15, 55, 168

This colorful midnight *milonga*, happening in the humble basement of the Armenian community center, sees dancers of all ages crowding the floor. La Viruta is friendly and atmospheric, a must-see for tango enthusiasts. See p138.

**Javier Gover**
*Creator & director of Wicked magazine*

**What does your magazine cover?** *Wicked* is a platform for emerging and alternative artists in Buenos Aires. It's a publication dedicated to the expression of art in the broadest sense – to the music, literature and visual art that pushes the boundaries of convention. **Where's the coolest street art?** My favorite mural at the moment is at Ciudad Cultural Konex (p108). A group of artists have also done beautiful work in Puerto Madero's Faena Art District (see p136). These works are always collaborative; there's not just one artist to credit. **What's cutting edge right now on the bar and restaurant circuit?** Il Ballo del Mattone (p120) combines excellent gastronomy with authentic art; the owners have commissioned graffiti-style art both inside and outside their restaurants in the up-and-coming Little Italy section of Palermo. For drinks, I like Caracas (p123) – it's elegant but not pretentious – and the Home Hotel bar (p123). They bring great DJs to their patio in summertime.

### ✪ LOS CARDONES *Peña*

☎ 4777-1112; www.cardones.com.ar, in Spanish; Jorge Luis Borges 2180, Palermo Viejo; 🕑 from 8.30pm Wed-Sat; 🚌 34, 36, 55, 93; Ⓜ Line D Plaza Italia

A cheap and cheerful *peña* (folk-music venue) alive with regional music and free-flowing wine, Los Cardones is a welcome change of pace from the barrio's posturing cocktail bars and clubs. See also p19 for more info.

### ✪ NICETO CLUB

*Dance Club, Concert Venue*

☎ 4779-9396; www.nicetoclub.com, in Spanish; Niceto Vega 5510, Palermo Viejo; 🕑 from 1am Thu-Sat; 🚌 21, 93, 111, 151, 168

One of the city's biggest crowd-pullers, the can't-miss event at Niceto Club is Thursday night's **Club 69** (www.club69.com.ar), a subversive DJ extravaganza featuring gorgeously attired showgirls, dancing drag queens, futuristic video installations and off-the-wall performance art. On weekend nights, spin masters take the booth with blends of hip-hop, dancehall, electronic beats, cumbia, reggae, and folklore.

### ✪ SALON CANNING *Tango*

☎ 4832-6753; Av Scalabrini Ortiz 1331, Palermo Viejo; 🕑 classes 7-11pm Mon, Tue & Fri, 9-11pm Thu, *milonga* 11pm-4am Mon-Fri; 🚌 15, 29, 39, 57, 168

Salon Canning attracts a young, local crowd of *tangueros* to a variety of *milongas*. The place gets especially busy on Monday and Tuesday nights when tango DJs hit the turntables for the dynamic Parakultural event. See the website for details: www.parakultural.com.ar.

### ✪ SITGES *Gay Club*

☎ 4861-3763; www.sitgesonline.com.ar; Av Córdoba 4119, Palermo; 🕑 10.30pm-late Wed-Sun; 🚌 92, 140, 168

This spacious brick-walled club, illuminated by funky chandeliers and a blue-glowing bar, gets hectic on weekends when gay and lesbian partygoers drop by before heading to Glam (p101). Catch the amusing drag show on Wednesday nights.

# >LAS CAÑITAS & BELGRANO

On either side of Av del Libertador in the far north of the city are two neighborhoods that are close together on the map, but far apart in character. Las Cañitas is a trendy pocket of Palermo where the city's pretty young things drink and dance, while Belgrano, a green suburb-like barrio where porteño (BA local) families migrate when they need more space for the *niños* (children) to play, feels like BA's version of Brooklyn. Head to Belgrano to shop around the main thoroughfare, Av Cabildo, before stopping for tea in BA's tiny Chinatown. Save a trip to Las Cañitas for a day at the races – the city's polo grounds and horse racetrack border the neighborhood on the south side – or for a night on the town. Past the expensive loft-style apartments and fitness centers of Las Cañitas, Av Báez runs through a few dense blocks of fashionable sushi bars and rollicking pubs where rich local kids spill out onto the sidewalk, Coronas in hand, on balmy nights.

## LAS CAÑITAS & BELGRANO

### ⊙ SEE
Barrio Chino .................. **1** B1
Museo de Arte
   Español .................. **2** A1

### ⌂ SHOP
Anuva Vinos .................. **3** D3
Feria Modelo de
   Belgrano .................. **4** A2
Fundación Silataj .......... **5** A2
Valenti .................. **6** A2

### ⍓ EAT
Cantina Chinatown ....... **7** B1
Lotus Neo Thai .............. **8** B1
Moshi Moshi .................. **9** E3
Novecento .................. **10** E4

### ▽ DRINK
Kandi .................. **11** E3
Pipí-Cucú .................. **12** C4
Puerta Uno .................. **13** B1
Soul Café & Supersoul... **14** E4
Van Koning .................. **15** E3

### ★ PLAY
Campo Argentino
   de Polo .................. **16** F3
Hipódromo
   Argentino .................. **17** F3

# SEE

## BARRIO CHINO

**cnr Arribeños & Mendoza, Belgrano;
M Line D Juramento;** &

BA's petite but exuberant Barrio Chino (Chinatown), established by Taiwanese immigrants after WWII, is worth a visit for the great-value noodle and spring roll joints and exotic supermarkets where you can gawk at beheaded fish and pick up treats like lychee candy and beautifully packaged sake.

## MUSEO DE ARTE ESPAÑOL

☎ 4783-2640; www.museolarreta
.buenosaires.gov.ar, in Spanish;
Juramento 2291, Belgrano; admission $1,
free Thu ⏲ 1-7pm Mon-Fri, 10am-8pm
Sat & Sun; M Line D Juramento

Once the colonial home of modernist writer Enrique Larreta, the Museo de Arte Español (Museum of Spanish Art) now shows the author's personal collection of contemporary Spanish artwork.

# SHOP

## ANUVA VINOS *Wine*

☎ 4777-4661; www.anuvawines
.com; Av Luis Maria Campos 545, Las
Cañitas; ⏲ 10am-7pm Mon-Fri; 🚌 15,
29, 55

The business headquarters of Anuva Vinos, an upscale American-run wine club that conducts tastings at venues around town (see p16).

## FERIA MODELO DE BELGRANO *Market*

**Juramento 2527, Belgrano;** ⏲ 8am-1pm &
5:30-8pm Mon-Sat, 8am-1pm Sun; M Line
D Juramento

This antique covered market is a must for foodies. Dozens of stalls sell gourmet cheese, meat and produce; look for smoked wild boar from Patagonia, exotic wild mushrooms, trout from Bariloche and picture-perfect fruit.

## FUNDACIÓN SILATAJ
*Souvenirs, Handicrafts*

☎ 4785-8371; www.fundacionsilataj
.org.ar; Vuelta de Obligado 1933, Belgrano;
⏲ 9:30am-1pm & 3:30-8pm Mon-Fri,
9:30am-1pm Sat; M Line D Juramento

The hand-woven woolen mittens go for 30 pesos, but the fair-trade opportunity, as they say, is priceless. Fundación Silataj supports the indigenous artisans of northern Argentina. Go on a responsible shopping spree and pick up some gorgeous wooden serving dishes.

## VALENTI *Wine, Deli*

☎ 4783-0324; www.valenti.com.ar;
Vuelta de Obligado 1820, Belgrano;
⏲ 9am-9pm Mon-Sat & 10am-2pm Sun;
M Line D José Hernández

All the fixings for a gourmet picnic are on mouthwatering display here – exotic cheeses, cured Patagonian meats, pâté and wine sourced from small bodegas.

You'll find something wild to take home at Fundación Silataj

# 🍴 EAT

## 🍴 MOSHI MOSHI
*Sushi* $$$

☎ 4772-2005; www.moshi-moshi.com.ar, in Spanish; cnr Ortega y Gasset & Soldado de la Independencia 1707, Las Cañitas; ⏰ 8:30pm-late Tue-Sun; 🚌 15, 29, 55, 60, 64

Like the tasteful loft apartments that line the block, this posh 1st-floor Japanese restaurant is outfitted in white minimalist decor. The discerning Cañitas set comes here for fresh takes on tempura and noodles.

## 🍴 NOVECENTO
*International* $$$

☎ 4778-1900; www.novecento.com; cnr Av Báez & Argüibel, Las Cañitas;

⏰ 9am-late Mon-Fri, from 11am Sat & Sun; 🚌 15, 29, 55, 60, 64

Grilled steak, suckling pig, Asian-style stir-fry or an American-style breakfast with eggs and coffee – this smart, good-looking bistro pulls off an eclectic menu.

# 🍸 DRINK

## 🍸 KANDI *Bar, Club*

☎ 4772-2453; Av Báez 340, Las Cañitas; ⏰ 8pm-late; 🚌 15, 29, 59, 60, 64; ♿

This retro cocktail bar, with its caramel leather seating, round mirrors and wooden floors, is cool, design-wise, and a hit with the local hipsters who pile in after midnight.

## WHAT'S YOUR BEEF?

Your mouth waters, your pulse races, your mind reels: it must be your first time standing near the countless cuts of steak sizzling on the *parrilla* (grill). Easy there – the local carnivore culture isn't so complex when you learn the basics. Argentina's definitive steak is the *bife de chorizo* (sirloin; not to be confused with the sausage called simply *chorizo*). Other popular cuts include *bife de lomo* (tenderloin), the succulent *ojo de bife* (rib eye) and *bife ancho* (a boneless rib cut). *Churrasco*, a thin steak, is a favorite quick-fix meal for gauchos. Porteños like their beef cooked through, so if you like your steak a little juicier, ask for *jugoso* (rare) or *a punto* (medium-rare). Try adding some extra flavor to the meat with a dash of *chimichurri* (oil and herb sauce) and – need it be said? – be sure to wash down your red meat with a fine red wine.

### PIPÍ-CUCÚ *Bar, Club*
☎ 4551-9314; Ciudad de la Paz 557, Belgrano; ⏱ 10am-1am Mon-Sat; 🚌 42, 59, 152; ♿

Pipí-Cucú is a local expression meaning 'gorgeous.' This artistic cocktail bar and brasserie is fashionable and coolly understated: everything from the chairs to the wine glasses are mismatched.

### PUERTA UNO *Bar*
☎ 4706-1522; www.puertauno.com; Juramento 1667, Belgrano; ⏱ 9pm-late Mon-Sat; Ⓜ Line D Juramento

This seductive speakeasy is hidden – there's no sign – and features expertly prepared cocktails and beautiful people.

### SOUL CAFÉ & SUPERSOUL
*Bar, Club*
☎ 4778-3115; Av Báez 246/252, Las Cañitas; ⏱ 8pm-late Tue-Sun; 🚌 15, 29, 59, 60, 64; ♿

These 1970s-style sister bars are equally groovy. Soul Café is furnished with kitschy hanging dice lamps and stylish white seats, while Supersoul has curvy red walls, hanging disc 'curtains' and a long wall mirror that makes people-watching possible.

### VAN KONING *Bar*
☎ 4772-9909; www.vankoning.com; Av Báez 325, Las Cañitas; ⏱ 7pm-late; 🚌 15, 29, 59, 60, 64; ♿

When the barrio's bars leave you longing for something more, head to this Dutch-style pub for rustic dark-wood booths, candlelight and frosty pints of Otro Mundo (a local microbrew).

 PLAY

### CAMPO ARGENTINO DE POLO DE PALERMO *Sport*
☎ 4777-6444; www.aapolo.com, in Spanish; cnr Avs del Libertador 4300 &

## NOODLES & TEA

Buenos Aires' little Chinatown is the barrio to be in when you feel like trading your steak knife for a pair of *palitos* (chopsticks). Fried-rice-and-jasmine-tea purists favor traditional, family-run diners like the cheerful **Cantina Chinatown** ( ☎ 4783-4173; Cnr Arribeños & Mendoza; ☷ noon-midnight Tue-Sun) Plop down at a table by the corner window and order up tender *empanadas chinas a la plancha* (pot-stickers) and a deep, steaming bowl of rice noodle soup seasoned with delicious Argentina beef. Style-conscious types opt to dine at a more contemporary eatery like **Lotus Neo Thai** ( ☎ 4783-7993; www.lotusneothai. com; Arribeños 2265; ☷ 12-3:30pm Tue-Sun & 8pm-late daily), a Las Cañitas institution that recently made the move to Barrio Chino. Kick back with the heady, mint-infused house cocktail at this blissful Thai eatery where painted lotus flowers climb the walls and guests recline on floor cushions. The duck curry and pad thai, when requested, pack heat.

**Dorrego, Las Cañitas; admission $20-500;** 🚌 **15, 29, 55, 60, 64;** ♿

Argentina is deservedly famous for polo. A springtime match is more than a display of athletic prowess – it's a chance to watch BA's upper crust in action. The players' expensive haircuts and spiffy uniforms render them almost as elegant as the horses they rode in on.

### ▦ HIPÓDROMO ARGENTINO
*Sport*

☎ **4778-2800; www.palermo.com.ar, in Spanish; cnr Avs del Libertador 4101 & Dorrego, Las Cañitas; admission $10;** ☷ **Sat-Mon;** 🚌 **10, 37, 160;** ♿

A few hours at the horseraces in the glamorous grandstand of the historic Hipódromo Argentino is a fabulous afternoon outing. The big race of the season is the Gran Premio Nacional in November.

Buenos Aires is a vibrant metropolis crowded with architectural monuments, contemporary art galleries, tango halls, fashionable boutiques, traditional steakhouses, open-air antique markets, atmospheric old cafes, leather shops, stylish cocktail bars and lively nightclubs. Read up on the basics to expand your savoir faire before diving into the urban fray.

| | |
|---|---|
| > Accommodations | 136 |
| > Tango | 138 |
| > Music | 140 |
| > Food | 141 |
| > Bars | 142 |
| > Clubs | 143 |
| > Gay & Lesbian BA | 144 |
| > Fashion | 145 |
| > Estancias | 146 |
| > Art | 147 |
| > Sports | 148 |
| > Architecture | 149 |
| > Buenos Aires with Kids | 150 |

Floralis Genérica (p94) opens its metallic petals heavenward, Recoleta

# ACCOMMODATIONS

Prices are slowly but surely rising in Buenos Aires, and while steak and wine still seem like a steal to foreigners, nightly hotel rates are approaching those of any world capital. Still, you don't have to break the bank for a chance to fall asleep to the melancholy strains of tango music. Many of the city's smaller boutique hotels and guesthouses are both charming and fairly priced, while several of the grander hotels offer frequent web deals and weekend packages – and true budget travelers take their pick from a wide range of hostels competing for business by offering rooftop *asados* (barbecues) and wi-fi. Review your options before setting foot on Argentine soil to allow yourself the best possible range of options.

At the top of the accommodation food chain are the opulent Louis XIV-style **Alvear Palace Hotel** (www.alvearpalace.com) and the luxe **Palacio Duhau-Park Hyatt** (www.buenosaires.park.hyatt.com), both standing grandly on Recoleta's ritzy Av Alvear. Their gorgeous marble spas and white-gloved afternoon tea service ensure a first-class experience for visiting socialites and dignitaries. Rock stars and fashion models with pesos to spare usually opt instead for the **Faena Hotel + Universe** (www.faenahotelanduniverse.com), the sultry Philippe Starck–designed paradise in Puerto Madero.

Further down the chain are some of the city's most stylish sleeps – the cool contemporary boutique hotels of Palermo Viejo. Award-winning **Home Hotel** (www.homebuenosaires.com), thanks to a sleek pool bar and cutting-edge interior design, is usually booked far in advance. Newer boutique hotels like **Miravida Soho** (www.miravidasoho.com) and **Legado Mítico** (www.legado mitico.com) also draw a fashionable clientele who want to sleep in the vicinity of Palermo's happening art, fashion, and dining scene.

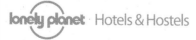 **lonely planet** · Hotels & Hostels

Need a place to stay? Find and book it at lonelyplanet.com. Over 60 properties are featured for Buenos Aires – each personally visited, thoroughly reviewed and happily recommended by a Lonely Planet author. From hostels to high-end hotels, we've hunted out the places that will bring you unique and special experiences. Read independent reviews by authors and other travelers, and get practical information including amenities, maps and photos. Then reserve your room simply and securely via Hotels & Hostels – our online booking service. It's all at lonelyplanet.com/hotels.

Shorter on design amenities but long on local character are the bohemian guesthouses and small hotels of San Telmo, like the lovely tango-themed **Mansíon Dandi Royal** (www.mansiondandiroyal.com) and the petite colonial-style **Posada de la Luna**. Ideally positioned for sightseeing in the Microcentro, Retiro, Puerto Madero and La Boca, San Telmo's accommodations are housed in historic buildings and situated nearby neighborhood *parrillas* (grill restaurants) and cafes.

Innumerable midrange hotels are scattered across the city, offering standard accommodations and myriad mod cons to business travelers and families; apartment-style hotels like **Art Suites** (www.artsuites.com.ar) are great value. Similarly widespread are Buenos Aires' various hostels, offering communal space and some private rooms to young travelers and backpackers. Try **Kapake Palermo Hostel** (www.kapake.com.ar) in Palermo Viejo or, on the south side of the city, San Telmo's cool **Ostinatto** (www.ostinatto.com).

Hotel staff throughout Buenos Aires are usually happy to help you arrange Spanish classes or book a tango show – just ask. No matter where you stay, taxis are cheap, plentiful and fast. Usually it takes no more than 20 minutes and costs around $20 to travel from Palermo to San Telmo – the Subte, depending on traffic, is often even faster.

## MOST UNIQUE SLEEPS

> Faena Hotel + Universe (www.faena hotelanduniverse.com)
> Mansíon Dandi Royal (www.mansion dandiroyal.com)
> Legado Mítico (www.legadomitico.com)
> Hotel Boca Juniors (www.hotelboca juniors.com)

## BEST BOUTIQUE HOTELS

> Home Hotel (www.homebuenosaires .com)
> Tailor Made Hotel (www.tailormade hotels.com.ar)
> Five Cool Rooms (www.fivebuenos aires.com)
> 1555 Malabia House (www.malabia house.com.ar)
> Bo Bo Hotel (www.bobohotel.com)

## MOST BANG FOR YOUR BUCK

> Abode (www.abodebuenosaires.com)
> The Four Hotel (www.thefourhotel .com.ar)
> Posada de la Luna (www.posadaluna .com)
> Che Lulu Trendy Hotel (www.luluguest house.com)
> La Otra Orilla (www.otraorilla.com.ar)

## BEST FOR DESIGN GEEKS

> Moreno 376 (www.morenobueno saires.com)
> Miravida Soho (www.miravidasoho. com)
> cE Design (www.designce.com)
> 248 Finisterra (www.248finisterra .com)
> Craft Hotel (www.crafthotel.com)

# TANGO

Some days at sunset, the whole of Buenos Aires seems to be moving to the rhythm of a tango soundtrack – old gents deal cards in corner bars while Carlos Gardel's voice wafts out of a transistor radio, a child plays the *bandoneón* (accordion) for tourists on the Subte, and local dancers warm up for a nightly *milonga* (social dance) as the beat-up sound system plays tango classics. The iconic dance and musical form are experiencing a revival in Buenos Aires. Not only do the nostalgic old tango dancers have a renewed sense of pride in the tradition, foreigners are doubly entranced by the melancholic tango. Walk past the Sunday night *milonga* in San Telmo's Plaza Dorrego (p73) and you'll see eager young travelers putting their first tango lessons to the test, dancing cheek-to-cheek with distinguished-looking partners three times their age. Social dances in tango dance halls are particularly popular, and while the afternoon *milonga* at Confitería Ideal (p45; pictured right) attracts a sizable crowd, the Saturday night *milonga* (which runs until 4am) is packed.

For many years, tango was despised by the porteño (BA local) elite and considered a vulgar pastime of the working class. The dance had humble beginnings, to be sure. It got going at the end of the 19th century in Buenos Aires' brothels, where a melting pot of poor immigrants and country folk danced together while waiting their turn to slip behind the bedroom door. The tango drew on stylistic influences from African, Spanish, Italian and traditional Argentine dance forms. Developed by men who had left their families behind to start a life in Argentina's bustling capital city, the dance expressed machismo, passion, longing and a fighting edge – and was set to an emerging sound rooted in Spanish and Italian melodies, *criollo* (Argentine-born) verse and Afro-Uruguayan *candombe* (a drum-based rhythm).

When Argentine musicians took tango to Paris at the beginning of the 20th century, it quickly swept through the ballrooms of Europe. By 1913, everyone wanted to dance the tango, and only then did the porteño aristocrats embrace the trend in the upscale dance halls of Recoleta. In 1917, Carlos Gardel (see the boxed text, p56) recorded the poetic 'Mi Noche Triste' (My Sad Night). Considered the genre's first anthem, it featured Gardel's crooning, charismatic voice and set a new standard – laments of lost love, faraway mothers and changing barrios would become the musical expression of the porteño psyche.

The genre continued to transform throughout the following decades with the introduction (and later decline) of orchestras. By the 1970s, the legendary Astor Piazzolla, a master on the *bandoneón*, was moving tango out of the dance halls and blending the form with jazz and classical music in international music venues. After the economic crisis of 2001, former rocker Daniel Melingo experimented with adding a harder edge to tango and trading the old-fashioned text for contemporary lyrics. Music collectives Bajofondo Tango Club (now known simply as Bajofondo) and Paris-based Gotan Project ignited tango electrónica, an energetic and sensual music form that's become extremely popular in Buenos Aires and abroad.

If tango tops your must-do list, start by seeing a tango show or stopping by a *milonga*. Private and group lessons are available in dance halls and advertised throughout the city. For more information on tango travel, packages, tours, shows, lessons and *milongas*, check out the following websites: www.tangobuenosaires.gov.ar (the official Argentine government tango portal); www.buenosairesmilongas.com (comprehensive listing of local *milongas*); and www.argentinatango.com, www.tangoaficionado.com and www.triptotango.com (informative foreign sites offering tango package tours and listing BA *milonga* venues).

**BEST TANGO SHOWS**
> El Querandí (p83)
> El Viejo Almacén (p83)
> Bar Sur (p82)
> 36 Billares (p59)
> La Cumparsita (p83)

**BEST MILONGAS**
> Confitería Ideal (p45)
> Salon Canning (p127)
> El Beso (p60)
> Centro Region Leonesa (p61)
> La Viruta (p125)

# MUSIC

Buenos Aires is alive with the sound of music – with melancholy tango melodies, yes, but also with lively *rock nacional* (Argentine rock), seductive tango electrónica, operatic arias, DJ-spun *cumbia* (Colombian-born beats popularized in the slums of BA) and folk music from the north like the *chamamé* and *chacarera*. Whether you'd prefer to kick back at a jazz club or listen to guitar-strumming gauchos, don't miss a nighttime sojourn into Buenos Aires' colorful music scene.

The nation's great unifying force could well be *rock nacional*, a mainstream rock-and-roll genre – porteño mechanics and businessmen alike know the words to hits produced by Charly García and his trailblazing '70s group Sui Generis. The uber-popular 1980s outfit Soda Stereo paved the way for today's headliners, from rock groups like Divididos and Fito Páez to the clever folk-pop troubadour Kevin Johansen.

*Rock nacional* songwriters who experimented with ethnic forms heralded the popular revival of Argentine *folklórica* (folk music). This evocative blend of traditional Andean music and European rhythms, pioneered by the masterful Mercedes Sosa, is performed nightly at *peñas* (folk venues) across the city.

The city's grand theaters provide glamorous settings for the flourishing classical music scene, while jazz is on at smoky subterranean bars and a string of nightclubs host innovative DJs spinning Latin gangster beats for the younger set. Tango fans can hear *orquestas típicas* (tango orchestras) performing in *milongas* – or have a listen to something fresher, the dramatic tango electrónica. See the agenda at www.whatsupbuenos aires.com for music listings.

## BEST FOR A LITTLE NIGHT MUSIC
> Thelonious Club (p111)
> Los Cardones (p127)
> La Peña del Colorado (p111)
> Notorious (p101; pictured right)
> Centro Cultural Torquato Tasso (p82)

# FOOD

Little more than a decade ago, basic steak, pasta and pizza were the extent of Argentine cuisine – but recently, the city's gastronomic horizons have widened considerably. A well-traveled generation of savvy restaurateurs and talented chefs have brought their newfound know-how to the dinner table, offering fresh takes on classic Argentine dishes. Factor in the supreme quality of Argentina's meat and produce (and the still-favorable exchange rate for many tourists) and voilà! You're in foodie heaven.

Many of the city's most stylish and adventurous restaurants are in Palermo Viejo. The barrio's cobblestoned streets are mobbed at night by well-dressed porteños sharing tapas at sidewalk tables and parading into bustling brasseries, seductively lit Thai eateries, and high-class sushi bars. A few upmarket *parrillas* also draw a discerning local crowd, though your best bet for steak with local character is further south in the San Telmo barrio. These classic restaurants could often use a lick of paint – you won't find polished concrete floors or mood music here – but these inexpensive old-time eateries feed the city's soul with brilliant beef fresh from the grill (see p22). The perfect accompaniment to this carnivore's delight is, of course, an outstanding Argentine Malbec (see p16).

The only downside for jetlagged visitors is that porteños eat late. Restaurants rarely open for dinner before 8pm, and tables don't start filling up until after 10pm. Dinner is a leisurely affair, so you'll get to bed late and rise as the locals do with a breakfast of *medialunas* (pastries) and coffee.

## BEST STEAK DINNER
> Don Julio (p120)
> Parrilla 1880 (p78)
> La Dorita (p120; pictured right)
> Miranda (p121)
> Gran Parrilla del Plata (p77)

## BEST CONTEMPORARY CUISINE
> 788 Food Bar (p98)
> La Vinería de Gualterio Bolívar (p77)
> Sagardi Euskal Taberna (p78)
> Café San Juan (p76)
> Green Bamboo (p120)

**v**

SNAPSHOTS

# BARS

Porteños love to get dolled up and hit the town, but you won't see any locals getting plastered at the corner bar. The natives don't imbibe much compared with Europeans and North Americans – maintaining composure is a point of pride – so it stands to reason when they go out for a drink (that's right, one drink), they don't bother with cheap beer or shots of vodka. Locals generally opt for microbrews, cocktails made with fresh fruit juice, or a glass of Malbec when they meet friends for happy hour or late-night drinks on the weekend. On weekdays, the bar scene gets going after work as young businessmen loosen their ties at wine bars like Gran Bar Danzon (p98) and a casual bohemian set goes for beers and *picadas* (cheeses, meats and olives served on a wooden breadboard) at low-key watering holes like Dadá (p69) or El Federal (p80). After dinner, cool and moody venues like La Cigale (p43; pictured below) and Mundo Bizarro (p124) see a round of hand-holding couples and groups of friends. The spirits start flowing much later on Friday and Saturday nights – many venues are still near-empty at midnight – when locals bar-hop through the open-air terraces and intimate lounges of Palermo Viejo. The fashionable barrio, home to hot spots like Carnal (p123), Bar 6 (p123) and Casa Cruz (p123), hums with nightlife; many of the city's most talented bartenders mix their inventive concoctions here for a mellow, good-looking crowd. The locals certainly aren't afraid to burn the candle on both ends – unless you're a night owl, you probably won't be around for the last call.

### BEST FOR LAID-BACK DRINKS
> Dadá (p69)
> Bar Seddón (p79)
> Pipí-Cucú (p132)
> Van Koning (p132)
> La Cigale (p43)

### BEST FOR EXOTIC COCKTAILS
> Milión (p99)
> 647 (p79)
> Le Bar (p44)
> Casa Cruz (p123)
> Ølsen (p121)

# CLUBS

With a reputation for long nights and early mornings, Buenos Aires has always had a thumping club scene. When house music took the world by storm in the late 1980s, followed by techno in the '90s, dance clubs opened all over the city, including an outpost of legendary Pachá (p122; pictured below). Porteño Hernán Cattaneo became Pachá's resident DJ in 1996, and was soon spinning alongside big names such as Paul Oakenfold, John Digweed, Dave Seaman and Sasha. Now Cattaneo is one of the world's hottest DJs, and porteños nod with approval when they see posters plastered on walls promoting dance parties he's headlining.

As a general rule, Buenos Aires' clubs don't open their doors before midnight, and most porteños don't start lining up until 2am. Most clubs don't close until morning, usually between 7am and 9am, so bring some sunglasses for the next day. Take small notes for taxis too (never hand over a $100 note), as clubs are scattered around the city. Entry fees range from $15 to $50, though prices run a lot higher for major dance events. Serious clubbers should focus their energies on Costanera Norte clubs (p122), while those looking to get home before the sun comes up should check out more laid-back venues like El Living (p59) or the Basement Club (p101).

Check out www.surfacebookings.com.ar for DJ tours and dance events and links; and www.buenosaliens.com for comprehensive links and listings of DJs, clubs, events, music companies and DJ gear.

**BEST UP-ALL-NIGHT CLUBS**
> Crobar (p110)
> Niceto Club (p127)
> Cocoliche (p45)
> Club Aráoz (p110)
> Pachá (p122)

**BEST FOR A FEW HOURS ON THE TOWN**
> Museum (p83)
> El Living (p59)
> Basement Club (p101)
> Asia de Cuba (p51)
> Maluco Beleza (p60)

# GAY & LESBIAN BA

Progressive Buenos Aires is one of Latin America's gay capitals and a city that's open to alternative lifestyles (what else would you expect of a culture built on tango, a sensual dance originally performed by a pair of men?). Argentina, after all, has recognized same-sex civil unions since 2003, and for World AIDS Day 2005 it boldly dressed its beloved Obelisco (p40) in a bright pink condom.

The queer scene ranges from establishments that are simply billed as 'gay-friendly' but attract a mixed clientele – like mellow Pride Café (p82) and **Palermo Viejo B&B** (www.palermoviejobb.com) – to heaving clubs complete with dancing boys and dark rooms, like Glam (p101), and South America's first five-star gay hotel, the flamboyant **Axel** (www.axelhotels.com). By comparison to the happening all-boys scene, the lesbian domain is quieter and more covert, but you'll find a high concentration of gay women at smaller hot spots like Bach Bar (p125).

Though Buenos Aires' thriving gay scene has been compared to that of San Francisco, there's no barrio here that's equivalent to the Castro – the local queer sphere is spread across San Telmo, Retiro, Barrio Norte and Palermo Viejo. Navigate the rainbow flag-waving scene through a gay travel agency like **Pride Travel** (www.pride-travel.com) or **Step Gay** (www.stepgay.com). Pick up the excellent *Gay Map* (an interactive version is at www.gaymaps .org), available for free in bars and hotels and highlighting gay-friendly restaurants, bars, cinemas, spas and shops.

## BEST GAY-FRIENDLY EATERIES
> Pride Café (p82)
> Empire Thai (p67)
> Cluny (p119)

## BEST GAY & LESBIAN CLUBS
> Club 69, Niceto Club (p127)
> Bulnes Class (p110)
> Glam (p101)
> Sitges (p127)

# FASHION

Buenos Aires is overrun with high-fashion boutiques and multibrand showrooms where the racks are crammed with designs by up-and-coming trendsetters. Prices have risen in recent years, but the city's still a shopper's playground rife with fashionable and (relatively) affordable trench coats, avant-garde cocktail dresses, slim-cut wool sweaters and leather boots that will inspire your friends back home to book a plane ticket to Argentina faster than the salesperson can say 'Visa or Mastercard?'

Palermo Soho is the beating heart of the city's high fashion scene and home to the flagship boutiques of designers like Cora Groppo (p113) and Nadine Zlotogora (p117). Upscale shopping centers like Alto Palermo (p107) also stock these designer lines, but you'll have to head to the boutiques along Recoleta's exclusive Av Alvear to find the true height of luxury. Discover more mainstream fashion along Av Santa Fe, the low-key streets of San Telmo, and the weekend designer fair circling Palermo's Plaza Serrano. Lusting after leather? Browse the shops in Retiro around Plaza San Martín and, if you have the patience for pushy salespeople, the leather stores along Microcentro's Florida and Lavalle streets. For a quieter scene and high-quality calf skin, head to Montserrat's leather outlets near the Mexico and San José intersection.

Check out the fashion section of the official **Buenos Aires tourism site** (www.bue.gov.ar) for more on recommended shopping venues and **Fashion Buenos Aires** (www.buenosairesmoda.com) for a comprehensive list of designers. Also look for excellent (and free) shopping maps of the city's various neighborhoods, available in businesses around town.

### BEST FOR HER
> Juana de Arco (p117)
> Nadine Zlotogora (p117)
> Rapsodia (p118; pictured right)
> Josefina Ferroni (p96)
> Cora Groppo (p113)

### BEST FOR HIM
> Felix (p116)
> Tramando (p97)
> Pablo Ramírez (p75)
> 28 Sport (p113)
> Hermanos Estebecorena (p117)

SNAPSHOTS

# ESTANCIAS

Where have all the cowboys gone? You might find a gaucho getting rowdy in one of the city's *peñas*, but if you want to see some real silver spurs and leather chaps, you'll have to head for wide open spaces. The flat, rolling countryside surrounding the capital is dotted with ranches where you can encounter cowboy culture and gallop into the sunset astride an Argentine thoroughbred.

Dozens of *estancias*, or rural estates that were once the private getaways of wealthy porteño families, have opened their picket fences to the public. Many of these country hotels offer a *día de campo* (country day) that's ideal for day-trippers. One of the friendliest and most authentic options within easy reach of Buenos Aires is Estancia Los Dos Hermanos. You'll roll up to the farm for a country breakfast before mounting a horse and following the estancia's resident gaucho into the fields for a morning ride. Then it's back to the farmhouse for an alfresco *asado* (barbecue) and a quick hammock siesta before you hit the trails again for a few whiplash-inducing hours on horseback.

Rather hang your hat near the stables than race back to the city? *Estancia* accommodations range from luxurious suites with private fireplaces to rustic rooms with hardwood floors. Do your homework at www .estanciasargentinas.com – some *estancias* are just private homes that begrudgingly rent rooms for profit, others are campy circuses that bring in buses of camera-snapping tourists – but don't miss a chance to live out your cowboy dreams in the Argentine pampas.

## BEST FOR A DAY TRIP
> Los Dos Hermanos (www.estancia losdoshermanos.com)
> La Figura (www.estancialafigura.com.ar)
> El Ombú de Areco (www.estancia elombu.com)

## BEST FOR A COUNTRY WEEKEND
> Candelaria del Monte (www.candel ariadelmonte.com.ar)
> Mestiza Pampa Lodge (www.mestiza lodge.com)
> Juan Gerónimo (www.juangeronimo .com.ar)
> El Vinten (www.elvinten.com.ar)

# ART

Porteño painters aren't exactly short on artistic inspiration. The clash of European and indigenous cultures, the aftermath of a brutal military government, the economic collapse of 2001 – local creative minds can take their pick from any number of hardships. Despite little support from the government, porteño artists are producing more provocative work than ever before.

Major museums like MALBA (p105) and the Museo Nacional de Bellas Artes (p86) are classic art venues, but most of the city's cutting-edge creations are on display in smaller galleries. Traditionally, the scene has been centered in Recoleta, with venues like Isabel Anchorena (see the boxed text, p94) attracting an old-school crowd of art patrons, though the circuit has expanded to include newer Palermo galleries as well, like Braga Menéndez (p60). The most important gallery, Fundación Proa (p86), is way off the beaten path in La Boca. Younger, edgier galleries can be found in San Telmo, like Zavaleta Lab (p60), and in Palermo Viejo. Excellent video and sculpture exhibits often occur, as well, at cultural centers like Centro Cultural Recoleta (p93).

**What's Up Buenos Aires** (www.whatsupbuenosaires.com) takes tourists into paint-splattered artists' workshops for a behind-the-scenes view. Also see www.arteamundo.com for exhibit reviews and pick up the *Mapa de las Artes* (Buenos Aires Arts Map), available at art museums, for the most comprehensive exhibition listings.

## BEST ART MUSEUMS & CENTERS

> MALBA (p105)
> Museo Nacional de Bellas Artes (p94)
> Centro Cultural Borges (p39)
> Centro Cultural Recoleta (p93)
> Museo Nacional de Arte Decorativo (p106)

## MOST HAPPENING GALLERIES BY BARRIO

> Fundación Proa (p86), La Boca
> Zavaleta Lab (p60), San Telmo
> Ruth Benzacar (p60), Microcentro
> Daniel Abate (p94), Recoleta
> Braga Menendez Arte Contemporáneo (p60), Palermo Viejo

# SPORTS

Monday night *fútbol*? Please – soccer is a household topic every day of the week in Buenos Aires. Virtually every man, woman and child in the city is fiercely loyal to one of two rival teams, River Plate or Boca Juniors, and the capital practically shuts down when they face off during the periodic Súperclasico match. Venture into the crowd of *barra brava* (soccer hooligans) with a tour operator like **Tangol** (www.tangol.com) that will make sure you're not sitting in the wrong section.

    But there's more to local athletics than turf and penalty kicks. Argentina's national game, *pato* (duck; www.fedpato.com.ar), sees two teams of four men on horseback trying to throw a leather ball with handles (confused yet?) through a hoop at either end of a field. The nation's more famous for polo – and, admittedly, for the handsome polo players who star in Ralph Lauren print ads across the globe. Of course these upper-crust hunks have more to offer than chiseled cheekbones – their elegant horseback sport is on display at the Campo Argentino de Polo (p132) from September to mid-November. Similarly upper-class horseracing competitions are held at the historic Hipódromo Argentino (p133) – the spectators, gentlemen in tweed, couldn't be further removed the scrappy fans at La Bombonera (p12).

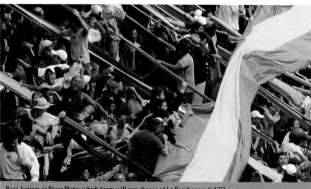

Boca Juniors or River Plate: which team will you choose at La Bombonera (p12)?

# ARCHITECTURE

You don't have to know the difference between a cornice and a cantilever to see that Buenos Aires is an architectural wonderland. In this melting-pot South American capital, no one style prevails – thanks to a mix of influences from the Old World, art-nouveau apartment buildings rise up beside Italian Renaissance-style palaces.

The experimentation began when Argentina declared independence from Spain in 1816. Proud porteños rejected Spanish culture, which explains the city's relative dearth of colonial architecture except for a few examples like the Cabildo (p38) on Plaza de Mayo. Defiant architects adapted aesthetics from elsewhere in Europe – Italy, France and ancient Greece – to build the city's most magnificent structures. Teatro Colón (p60) was influenced by German, French and Italian Renaissance styles, while Mario Palanti borrowed both thematic and structural inspiration from his native Italy to build Palacio Barolo (p54). The famed Juan Buschiazzo added Doric columns to the entrance of the Cementerio de la Recoleta (p93) and an Italian facade to the Mercado de San Telmo (p74); meanwhile, many of the city's art-deco buildings display Latin American flair, like Otto Wulf's 1912 building on the corner of Perú and Belgrano in Montserrat, which features Indian figures and Argentine fauna.

The result of this haphazard design scheme is a thoroughly cosmo-politan, indigenous, nationalist architecture. The grandest stretch of jaw-dropping buildings, built between 1880 and 1930, runs along Av de Mayo. Start at Palacio del Congreso (p54) – don't miss the fabulous, decaying El Molino (p54) on the corner – and meander towards Plaza de Mayo.

## MUST-SEE ANTIQUE STRUCTURES

> Palacio de las Aguas Corrientes (p54)
> Palacio Barolo (p54)
> Edificio Kavanagh (p64; pictured right)
> Mercado de Abasto (p108)

## COOLEST CONTEMPORARY DESIGN

> Puente de la Mujer (p48)
> Floralis Genérica (p94)
> Faena Hotel + Universe (p51)
> Museo Xul Solar (p94)

# BUENOS AIRES WITH KIDS

If the happy families and beautiful pregnant women crowding the streets of Buenos Aires are any indication, porteños adore children. Unlike in many cities, you won't be the object of disapproving glares if you deign to bring your little one into a 'nice' restaurant, and the city, though hectic and often filthy, abounds with children's activities and lovely parks where *los niños* (children) can let loose.

On weekends, Palermo fills with families. Popular activities include feeding the zany koi fish at the Jardín Japonés (p104), catching an astronomy show at the Planetario Galileo Galilei in the Parque 3 de Febrero (p107), and hitting up the petting zoo at the Jardín Zoológico (p104; pictured below). Shopping malls are like stroller-derbies on rainy days, and Abasto (p108) not only has great kids' shops, it also has the fantastic Museo de los Niños, filled with interactive activities to keep little hands occupied.

Whether or not a children's menu is offered, most cafes and restaurants welcome children and offer freshly squeezed juices, hot chocolate, and simple, kid-friendly foods like pizza and spaghetti. If you'd rather not subject fellow diners to the baby's crying, seek the company of other kid-toting families at eateries like the cafe at **Recursos Infantiles** (www.recursos infantiles.com.ar) or restaurants like **La Payuca** (www.lapayuca.com) that offer babysitter-staffed playrooms. Remember, porteños eat dinner late, but you can always pick up fresh fruit and *empanadas* between meal times.

Navigating Buenos Aires with kids, whether on foot or public transport, requires planning. Strollers are hard to steer through the busy sidewalks, buses are crowded, taxis are cramped – but rest assured, there's always a temper-taming ice-cream shop at your destination.

## BEST KID-FRIENDLY SPOTS
> Jardín Zoológico (p104)
> Planetario Galileo Galilei at Parque 3 de Febrero (p107)
> Reserva Ecológica (p49)

A street vendor at La Boca's Caminito (p86)

# BACKGROUND

## HISTORY

As the capital of Argentina, Buenos Aires' history is inseparable from that of the country – a tumultuous history of dictatorships and democracy, prosperity and poverty.

### BUENOS AIRES TODAY

Buenos Aires lives with the scars of several economic crashes, most notably the collapse in 2001. Hardworking professionals lost their savings, families had to give up their houses and move into smaller apartments, and national pride was damaged as Argentina's international status tumbled. Things started to look up for Buenos Aires residents after the election of ex-president Nestor Kirchner, who restructured Argentina's debt and brought sustainable growth to the country during his 2003–2007 term. Kirchner endeavored to reconcile the country with its past, revoking the immunity of officials who participated in the military government of 1976–82 and facilitating trials of war criminals. The investigations and trials continue.

Kirchner's wife, former senator Cristina Fernández de Kirchner, succeeded her husband as Argentina's president in October 2007. Though she's continued the economic programs her husband started, she's often perceived as a controversial figure who's spent much of her professional energy battling the province's farmers over taxation issues and trying to maintain social stability in the face of inflation and skyrocketing job losses, partly caused by the international economic crisis that began in 2008. She is up for re-election in October 2011 and is likely to win.

Meanwhile, the Madres of Plaza de Mayo (see also p17) continue their campaign to identify the children of the *desaparecidos* (disappeared ones). During the military government, the military captured (and later murdered) thousands of young parents, whose babies were then distributed among military families. Many of these children (now in their 30s) are unaware of their own lineage. Newspaper notices urge people with any suspicions about their parentage to come forward and begin the process of investigating their own family history. Though a handful of these children of the *desaparecidos* have uncovered the truth and been reunited with their actual relatives, many are understandably reluctant to acknowledge any such suspicions, and the subject remains a tense one.

## BACKWATER PORT TURNS CAPITAL

Buenos Aires was founded twice. Spaniard Pedro de Mendoza's 1536 settlement failed after settlers were ousted by the indigenous Querandí, who had populated the Río de la Plata banks for tens of thousands of years. Juan de Garay re-established Buenos Aires in 1580, though it remains unclear exactly where in the city he planted the Spanish flag.

The town remained a backwater as the Spanish Crown focused its empire-building on silver-rich Alto Perú, restricting trade through Buenos Aires. As a result, local merchants turned to contraband. By 1776, the increasing wealth passing through the port finally forced Spain to make BA the capital of the new Viceroyalty of the Río de la Plata.

## INDEPENDENCE & THE GOLDEN AGE

The British attempted to claim Buenos Aires in 1806 and 1807, but the locals beat them back to their ships, pouring cauldrons of boiling oil and water from rooftops and firing cannons from balconies. The successful expulsion gave *criollos* (Argentine-born colonists) new confidence to stand up to Spain, and they declared independence on May 25, 1810. Formal independence for Argentina was declared in Tucumán on July 9, 1816.

After a lengthy civil war, a succession of presidents and the creation of Argentina's constitution, the country moved into a golden age of prosperity that lasted from the late 1800s until 1929. During this time, many fine buildings were built. Between 1869 and 1895, European immigrants flooded in, increasing the city's population sevenfold. Industry was unable to absorb this mass immigration and labor unrest grew. With the onset of the Great Depression, the military took power under conditions of considerable social unease.

## PERÓN TO ALFONSÍN

Juan Perón, with help from his charismatic wife, Eva (Evita) Perón (p93), became president in 1946. While the power couple had their critics, the Peróns also championed working-class causes and introduced social justice and welfare. Criticism regarding Perón's dictatorial demeanor, economic difficulties and Evita's 1952 death undermined Perón's second presidency, and in late 1955 a military coup exiled him to Spain, initiating nearly three decades of catastrophic military rule.

Perón returned to Argentina in 1973, became president again, and died a year later. On March 24, 1976, a military coup took control of the government, bringing General Jorge Videla to power and beginning a period of military goverment. In late 1980 Videla stepped down in favor of army general Roberto Viola, who served a year.

By 1982, the military dictatorship began to lose legitimacy, and in an attempt to drum up support, the government launched an invasion to dislodge the British from the Falkland Islands, which Argentina claimed as its own. Underestimating a strong British response, Argentina surrendered after 74 days. The military regime was left in tatters and civilian Raúl Alfonsín was elected president in 1983. Human-rights groups estimate that some 30,000 people were killed or 'disappeared' during the military dictatorship between 1976 and 1983.

## THE CRASH & ITS AFTERMATH

Carlos Ménem succeeded Alfonsín in 1989, inheriting hyperinflation and a recession. Ménem ushered in a 'golden age' of false economic stability, largely thanks to pegging the peso to the US dollar. By 2001 the economy teetered on collapse. Amid nationwide protests over a government freeze on bank withdrawals, Ménem's successor, Fernando de la Rúa, resigned. Eduardo Duhalde, chosen as caretaker president in 2002, devalued the peso and announced that Argentina would default on its US$140 billion foreign debt. Nestor Kirchner won office in May 2003. He refinanced and later paid off Argentina's $9.5 billion debt, and presided over several years of economic growth. He died of a heart attack in 2010 during the presidency of his wife, Cristina Fernandez de Kirchner. Nestor had been expected to run again in 2011, but instead Cristina is up for re-election. Despite a tumultuous presidency, she is popular with the working class and likely to win.

# GOVERNMENT & POLITICS

Officially known as the Ciudad Autónoma de Buenos Aires, BA is the capital of Argentina. The title denotes its standing as an independent district (similar to Washington, DC). The provincial capital is La Plata, 60km east.

Traditionally Argentina's president appointed the mayor of Buenos Aires, but constitutional reform in 1996 permitted Fernando de la Rúa to become the city's first elected mayor. The following mayor, Aníbal Ibarra, was removed from office in 2006 for negligence after an inquiry into a nightclub blaze that killed almost 200 people. The current mayor, Mauricio Macri, was well-known before his election as the president of the Boca Juniors *fútbol* club. A capitalist and the son of an international entrepreneur, he has announced his future interest in running for the presidency.

Politics in Buenos Aires is also played out on the streets, most visibly manifesting itself in the almost-daily protests around Plaza de Mayo (p40). Generally peaceful, these protests are carried out by groups of *piqueteros* (picketers) who block city streets, making demands or commemorating political events.

# ECONOMY

When 'convertibility' (pegging the peso to the US dollar) was scrapped and the government announced it would convert bank accounts at a rate of 1.4 pesos per dollar, everyone with money still in Argentine banks lost over half their dollar value. For most Argentines, this was a disaster. Argentina's sizable middle class was ruined, and today almost half of BA's population lives below the poverty line. Although the employment rates have gone up a bit in the last few years, inflation has complicated the financial affairs of many porteños. At the end of April 2011, inflation was officially at 9.7%

Former president Nestor Kirchner finished restructuring Argentina's debt, and at the end of his term, the economy was looking strong. Growth slowed during the start of Cristina Fernández de Kirchner's presidency – and matters weren't helped any by the worldwide economic crisis that started at the end of 2008.

The socioeconomic problems caused by the huge divide between rich and poor remain unresolved, a fact that's on obvious display every evening at sunset. Just before the garbage trucks roll through the city, bands of *cartoneros* (poor porteños who scour garbage looking for cardboard, glass and other recyclables they can exchange for money) rifle through the trash bags waiting on the street.

# ENVIRONMENT

Considering that Argentina is home to pristine wine regions, the glaciers of Patagonia and pastures of grass-fed cows stretching as far as the eye can see, tourists might expect Buenos Aires to be more eco-friendly than it actually is. Despite its position at the mouth of the Río de la Plata, on the eastern edge of the vast Argentine grasslands known as the Pampas, Buenos Aires is a megacity suffering from various types of pollution and environmental problems resulting from overpopulation. Noise (honking cars and roaring buses) and air pollution are factors of everyday life. Fortunately, frequent rains clear the smoggy air. City streets are often

**TUMMY-TUCKS & TANGO**

If you have a friend who comes back from Buenos Aires looking refreshed, relaxed and – how to put this? – better endowed, she might not have simply been taking tango lessons. When Argentina's economic woes began, plastic surgery was already wildly popular with locals, and with surgery available at around a third of US and European costs, 'health tourism' is very popular. A trip usually consists of a few nights in Buenos Aires, followed by a procedure ranging from gluteoplasty to the ever-popular breast implants. You didn't think that *all* of the women here were naturally beautiful, did you?

smattered with dog poop, especially in the city's south, making for an occasionally slippery and smelly walk.

Buenos Aires' waterways – most visibly the Riachuelo in the barrio of La Boca – are contaminated by industry. Despite Argentina's self-sufficiency in petroleum and hydroelectricity, the government has promoted nuclear power since 1950. The city lacks an official recycling system, though a huge number of *cartoneros* make their living picking through city trash for anything they can sell to recycling centers.

# LIFE AS A PORTEÑO

Buenos Aires is one of Latin America's most cosmopolitan cities. Between 1870 and 1920, over six million people immigrated to Argentina, the majority settling in BA. Most came from Spain and Italy, and also from Britain, Portugal, France and Eastern Europe post-WWII, bringing with them food, football and music. Middle Eastern and Asian immigrants also arrived.

Catholicism remains the official religion and while most porteños don't attend mass, they dangle rosaries from their rearview mirrors and cross themselves when passing churches.

Porteños are remarkably friendly. Stopping someone to ask directions is normal and often leads to friendly conversation about your origin and why you're in Buenos Aires. Many porteños speak some English and love the chance to practice. Although BA is known for its fashionable residents, the look is surprisingly casual – the key is to look clean and neat, not like you just rolled out of bed and down to the corner coffee shop.

During introductions, women exchange cheek kisses (one on each) and men shake hands. Among friends, men kiss cheeks too. Always exchange pleasantries – a *buenos días* (good morning) or *buenas tardes* (good afternoon) at minimum – with people you meet in elevators and shops and with taxi drivers.

# ARTS

## ARCHITECTURE

Buenos Aires boasts a fascinating mix of architecture and is one of the world's best cities for design students and lovers of all things architectural. See p149 for more.

## LITERATURE

Argentina's capital has long been a literary city, with bookstores, newsstands, book fairs and authors aplenty and a wealth of elegant cafes where you can get lost in a good novel. The most fitting place to start your reading is Jorge Luis Borges (1899–1986), one of the 20th century's greatest writers. He penned fiction, nonfiction and poetry, much of which is set just outside his former home in Buenos Aires. His stories are amassed into the tome *Collected Fictions,* which is translated into English – look for the Norman Thomas di Giovanni translation, which is superior to the later one.

Another 20th-century great is the bohemian Julio Cortázar (1914–84), a porteño writer who defected to Paris – but not before his *Rayuela* (Hopscotch) was deemed a milestone in modern fiction. Cortázar's inventive, nonlinear narrative invites readers to choose between two paths. Also of the Borges generation is Ernesto Sábato (1911–), whose complex and uncompromising novels have profoundly influenced Argentine literature. Other notable porteño writers include Adolfo Bioy Casares and sisters Silvina and Victoria Ocampo.

José Hernández (1834–1886) wasn't a porteño, but he did write one of the country's most important books, *Martín Fierro* (1872), an epic poem about gaucho life. It's sold in a variety of languages.

## FURTHER READING

> *Asleep in the Sun* (2004; Adolfo Bioy Casares)
> *The Buenos Aires Affair* (1973; Manuel Puig)
> *Heartbreak Tango* (1969; Manuel Puig)
> *The Invention of Morel* (2003; Adolfo Bioy Casares)
> *Labyrinths: Selected Stories & Other Writings* (2007; Jorge Luis Borges)
> *On Heroes and Tombs* (1981; Ernesto Sabato)

## FILM

Argentina has a long cinematic tradition (producing its first film in 1897) and a history of cinematically sophisticated movies. In the 1930s and '40s, popular genres included *tangueras* (tango-centered musicals) and gaucho Western films. You'll see these available for purchase at street kiosks.

Films of the 1960s and '70s were politically radical, such as Fernando Solanas and Octavio Getino's powerful, four-hour leftist documentary *La Hora de los Hornos* (The Hour of the Furnaces; 1968). A more mellow Solanas won Best Director at Cannes in 1988 for his mesmerizing *Sur* (South), and acclaim for his documentary *La Dignidad de los Nadies* (Dignity of the Nobodies; 2005) about the impact of the economic crisis on everyday life. For an insight into the period of military government, see Luis Puenzo's *The Official Story* (1985), which won a Best Foreign-language Film Oscar.

Recent decades have seen a uniquely Latin American magic realism appear in films such as Eliseo Subiela's *Hombre Mirando al Sureste* (Man Facing Southeast; 1985), and melodramas by feminists such as María Luisa Bemberg and Lucrecia Martel. Martel's films *La Cienaga* (The Swamp; 2001) and *La Niña Santa* (The Holy Girl; 2004) offer insights into the complexities of Argentine relationships.

## MUSIC

Tango (see also p138) is the heart and soul of porteño music, but there are many styles of music worth exploring in BA. Argentina's folk music is called *folklórica*. Styles such as *chamamé, chacarera,* samba and the *carnavlito* are all beautiful mixes of traditional Andean music and old European rhythms. BA's many *peñas* (folk venues) are the places to hear

---

### MOVIE MEMENTOS

These award-winning contemporary films capture quotidian life in Buenos Aires. Some are available internationally, others you'll find in the city's music and book stores (all have subtitles):

> *Nueve Reinas* (Nine Queens; 2000) – Fabián Bielinsky
> *El Hijo de la Novia* (Son of the Bride; 2001) – Juan José Campanella
> *El Bonaerense* (2002) – Pablo Trapero
> *Historias Mínimas* (Minimal Stories; 2002) – Carlos Solin
> *Assassination Tango* (2002) – Robert Duvall
> *Crónica de una Fuga* (Chronicle of an Escape; 2006) – Adrian Caetano
> *Derecho de Familia* (Family Law; 2007) – Daniel Burman
> *¿Quién Dice Que es Fácil?* (Who Says it's Easy?; 2007) – Juan Taratuto

## ESSENTIAL BUENOS AIRES SOUNDS

These classic albums, available from most music stores, will make you feel like you're in Buenos Aires when you're back home and have the workaday blues.

> *The Best of Carlos Gardel* – Carlos Gardel
> *Tango: Zero Hour* – Astor Piazzola
> *Mercedes Sosa en Argentina* – Mercedes Sosa
> *Bajofondo Tango Club* – Bajofondo Tango Club
> *Soda Stereo* – Soda Stereo

this infectious music. Arguably the nation's greatest *folklórica* singer was Atahulapa Yupanqui, who influenced later *nueva canción* (new song movement) musicians including the astounding Mercedes Sosa and Los Chalchaleros.

Argentina has also had a rich rock-and-roll heritage (called *rock nacional*; national rock) dating back to the 1960s – check out the Beatles-esque Los Shakers. Musicians such as Fito Páez and Charlie García (one half of influential '70s folk-rock group Sui Generis) are national icons. In the 1980s, the hugely influential Soda Stereo was Argentina's version of The-Police-meets-Duran-Duran. Contemporary performers include Bersuit Vergarabat and Kevin Johansen (born in Alaska to an Argentine mother). Johansen's music is like Leonard Cohen fused with Argentine folk.

## VISUAL ART

Xul Solar (1887–1963) was one of Argentina's most visionary modern artists, his work aligned with fauvist, expressionist, constructivist and cubist movements. Another renowned painter was Antonio Berni (1905–81), a neofigurative and impressionist artist who painted everyday scenes exploring socioeconomic inequality. The Galerías Pacífico (p40) ceiling features his murals. Benito Quinquela Martín (1890–1977) was a popular artist who put the working-class barrio of La Boca on the artistic map, painting vivid scenes of port life. The former homes of both Quinquela and Solar are now museums displaying their work (see p86 and p94).

Argentina's 2001 economic crisis triggered a tidal wave of ideas and output from BA's contemporary artists, and while there's little public support, many are making a living through commercial galleries and foreign sales. There are scores of small galleries in San Telmo, Recoleta, Retiro and Palermo. For comprehensive gallery listings, pick up a copy of *Mapa de Las Artes* (BA Art Map) from MALBA (p105) or most other art museums.

# DIRECTORY
## TRANSPORTATION

Hoof it, hop on the bus, take a taxi or descend into the Subte (subway) system – there's no shortage of transportation options in Buenos Aires. While some options are more glamorous than others, all are reliable and cheap by international standards.

### ARRIVAL & DEPARTURE
### AIR

**Aeropuerto Internacional Ministro Pistarini** (EZE; ☎ 5480-6111; www.aa2000.com.ar), better known as Ezeiza, is where nearly all international flights arrive. Left luggage is available next to the Farmacity store on the ground floor of Level A.

Domestic flights and flights to/from Uruguay leave from **Aeroparque Jorge Newbery** (AEP; ☎ 5480-6111; www.aa2000.com.ar; Av Costanera Rafael Obligado, Costanera Norte), a short distance from downtown.

#### Ezeiza
Traveling the 35km from the airport to town takes about 45 minutes by cab or shuttle, and up to 1½ hours by bus.

## Transport Times Between Neighborhoods

|  | Microcentro | Puerto Madero | Congreso & Tribunales |
|---|---|---|---|
| **Microcentro** | n/a | walk 10min | walk 10min, Subte 5min |
| **Puerto Madero** | walk 10min | n/a | taxi 10-15min, Subte 5min |
| **Congreso & Tribunales** | walk 10min, Subte 5min | taxi 10-15 min, Subte 5min | n/a |
| **Retiro** | walk 5min | walk 10-15min | walk 10min, Subte 5min |
| **San Telmo** | walk 15min | walk 10-15min | walk 15-20min, taxi 5min |
| **La Boca** | taxi 15min, bus 25min | taxi 10min | taxi 15min |
| **Recoleta & Barrio Norte** | walk 15-20min, taxi 5-10min | taxi 15min | taxi 10min |
| **Palermo** | taxi 20min, Subte 15min | taxi 25min, Subte 20min | taxi 15-20min Subte 10-15min |

Public bus 86 ($1.50) makes the slow slog into town – only take it if you're really pinching pennies. You can catch the bus outside the Aerolíneas Argentinas terminal, a short walk from the international terminal. **Manuel Tienda León** (MTL; ☎ 0810-888-5366; www.tiendaleon.com) offers fast, fairly priced shuttle buses to/from downtown ($50) every 30 minutes. Hotel drop-off/pickup is free within the city center; if your hotel is elsewhere, take the service to/from the **downtown office** (Map p63, D2; ☎ 4314-3636; Av Madero 1299 at San Martín, Retiro). MTL's airport office sits directly outside customs.

Avoid the freestanding vehicles and people shouting 'taxi!' around the airport. Always take an official taxi or *remise* – these can be booked at stands in the arrival hall and will cost you about $130–$150.

### Aeroparque Jorge Newbery
Public buses 33 and 45 ($1.30) run to the center (don't cross the street when you exit the airport, take them going south). MTL shuttles also run to the center ($20). A taxi to the center costs about $35.

## BUS
Buenos Aires' **Retiro Bus Terminal** (Map p63, D1; ☎ 4310-0700; www.tebasa.com.ar,

| | Retiro | San Telmo | La Boca | Recoleta & Barrio Norte | Palermo |
|---|---|---|---|---|---|
| | walk 5min | walk 15min | taxi 15min, bus 25min | walk 15-20min, taxi 5-10min | taxi 20min, Subte 15min |
| | walk 10-15min | walk 10-15min | taxi 10min | taxi 15min | taxi 25min, Subte 20min |
| | walk 10min, Subte 5min | walk 15-20min, taxi 5min | taxi 15min | taxi 10min | taxi 15-20min, Subte 10-15min |
| | n/a | walk 25min, taxi 10min | taxi 20min | taxi 10min | taxi 10-15min, Subte 15min |
| | walk 25min, taxi 10min | n/a | taxi 10min | taxi 15min | taxi 20-25min |
| | taxi 20min | taxi 10min | n/a | taxi 20min | taxi 25min |
| | taxi 10min | taxi 15min | taxi 20min | n/a | walk 10-30min, taxi 5-15min |
| | taxi 10-15min, Subte 15min | taxi 20-25min | taxi 25min | walk 10-30min, taxi 5-15min | n/a |

in Spanish; Av Ramos Mejía 1680, Retiro) offers bus connections to/from cities in Argentina and most South American capitals. Hundreds of bus companies serve Retiro (not to be confused with nearby Estación Retiro train station) – head to the information desk or check the website for destination info. Long-distance buses range from comfortable to luxurious (*cama suite* class includes champagne and nearly fully reclining seats for overnight trips). Make sure you get a luggage claim ticket and be sure to tip the handler.

Retiro is walking distance from the north end of calle Florida; a cab from here to anywhere in the center costs around $20.

## BOAT

There are several river crossings between Uruguay and Buenos Aires via ferry or hydrofoil; some trips also involve buses. Ferries leave from the following locations:

**Buquebus Terminal** (Map p47, A2; ☎ 4316-6500; www.buquebus.com; Av Antártida Argentina & Córdoba, Puerto Madero).

**Colonia del Sacramento** Daily ferries (one-way from $103, three hours) and hydrofoils (one-way from $192, one hour), with direct bus connections to Montevideo (three hours more).

**Montevideo** Daily high-speed ferries from BA to Montevideo (one-way from $315, three hours).

**Punta del Este** Daily hydrofoils from BA to Colonia connecting with direct bus service to Punta del Este (one-way from $262, five hours) and daily high-speed ferries from BA to Montevideo connecting with direct bus service to Punta del Este (one-way from $362, five hours).

## TRAVEL DOCUMENTS

Passports must be valid for six months from date of entry.

## VISA

Nationals of Australia, USA, Canada, New Zealand and most Western European countries do not need visas to visit Argentina, and you are allowed to stay for 90 days. At the start of 2009, Argentina, like some other South American countries, instated a 'reciprocity fee' that

---

## CLIMATE CHANGE & TRAVEL

Travel – especially air travel – is a significant contributor to global climate change. At Lonely Planet, we believe that all who travel have a responsibility to limit their personal impact. As a result, we have teamed with Rough Guides and other concerned industry partners to support Climate Care, which allows people to offset the greenhouse gases they are responsible for with contributions to energy-saving projects and other climate-friendly initiatives in the developing world. Lonely Planet offsets all staff and author travel.

For more information, turn to the responsible travel pages on www.lonelyplanet .com. For details on offsetting your carbon emissions and a carbon calculator, go to www .climatecare.org.

charges incoming US tourists an amount similar to what Argentine citizens pay for an American visa (currently about US$140).

### RETURN/ONWARD TICKET

A return/onward ticket is officially required but rarely requested.

### DEPARTURE TAX

An international departure tax (US$30) is levied on flights leaving Argentina, a cost that's often included in the price of a plane ticket. If your ticket doesn't cover this tax, you'll be directed to pay the fee at a desk in the Ezeiza departures hall.

## GETTING AROUND

With an underground subway (the Subte), a 24-hour bus system and a plethora of affordable taxis, Buenos Aires is easy to get around. The capital is a very walkable city, but when you need to cover a sizeable distance, the Subte or a cab is your best bet. Relying on public transport requires a bit of initial study. In this book, the nearest Subte or bus line is noted after the Ⓜ or 🚌 icon for each listing.

### BUS

The city has a huge and complex *colectivo* (bus) system, but it's not particularly user-friendly for foreigners – stops aren't announced, you need several coins to ride, and if you don't have a good idea where you're getting off, the bus will fly right past your destination. The only way to make any sense of the system is to purchase a *Guia T* (bus guidebook), available at kiosks throughout the city. Locate your destination street in the index, flip to the indicated map page and grid box, then match a bus number from that box to your departure box, and you're off. Most rides cost around $1.30. Get on the bus with a handful of change and tell the driver the name of your stop, insert the coins into the machine and wait for a ticket to pop out. Coins are scarce in BA, making bus travel tricky – there's talk of starting a more contemporary card system that doesn't involve small change, but no progress had been made at the time of research. A high-speed Metrobus system was inaugurated as this book went to print'

### SUBTE

BA's **Subte** ( ☎ 0800-555-1616; www .subte.com.ar, in Spanish) opened in 1913 and is the quickest way to get around the city. In summer – and at rush hour – the cars are hot and crowded, so be sure to watch your valuables. Single-ride magnetic cards cost $1.10 and can be purchased at *boleterías* (ticket booths) in all Subte stations. To save time, buy a five- or 10-ride card, since queues can get backed up. At some stations, the tracks separate the platforms, so make sure of your direction before passing through the turnstiles. Trains operate between 5am and 10:30pm from Monday to Saturday; and from 8am to 10pm on Sunday. Service is frequent on weekdays, slower on weekends.

## TRAIN
For getting around the city, the only train that really comes in handy is the Mitre line, which makes getting from Retiro to Las Cañitas or Belgrano's Chinatown a snap. At the ticket window inside Estación Retiro (Map p63, C2) ask for tickets ($2) to Belgrano station on the Mitre line.

## TAXI & REMISE
BA's black-and-yellow taxis ply the city day and night; you rarely have to wait long to hail one. To avoid any trouble with counterfeit notes or dodgy drivers, hail a taxi with the words 'radio taxi,' indicating that the vehicle is part of a licensed agency. The starting fare is $4.90, and drivers should always use the *taxímetro* (taxi meter). Tipping is not expected, but leave the small change. Most rides within one area of the city cost around $20, up to around $40 across the city. Call **Pidalo** ( ☎ 4956-1200) or **Radio Taxi Premium** ( ☎ 4374-6666).

*Remises* (radio taxis) look like regular cars and don't have meters. They cost about the same

as street taxis, but you're less likely to get ripped off because the fare is always established beforehand. Most hotels and restaurants will call a *remise* for you; it's also a handy way to get to the airport. Try **Remises Blue** ( ☎ 4777-8888).

# PRACTICALITIES
## BUSINESS HOURS
General business hours for offices are from 8am to 5pm, Monday to Friday. Shopping centers generally operate from 10am to 10pm daily. Most stores stay open until 7pm or 9pm on weekdays, and open from 9am to 1pm or 2pm on Saturdays. Popular shopping areas such as Palermo open on Sundays as well. Most banks close by 4pm on weekdays, and are open on Saturdays from 9am to 1pm. Restaurants generally open daily from noon to 3:30pm for lunch, and from 8pm to midnight or later for dinner. Cafes are open from early morning until after 8pm, often much later. Tourist offices open from 8am or 9am to between 8pm and 10pm daily.

## DISCOUNTS
### STUDENT & YOUTH CARDS
The International Student Identity Card (ISIC) – available for US$16 through the student and discount travel agency **Asatej** (Map p37, B2; ☎ 4114-7500; www.asatej.net, in Spanish;

Room 320, 3rd fl, Galería Buenos Aires, Florida 835, Microcentro; ☽ 9am-7pm Mon-Fri) – can help travelers obtain discounts on museum admissions.

## SENIORS' DISCOUNTS

Travelers over the age of 60 can sometimes obtain senior-citizen discounts on museum admissions and the like. Usually a passport with date of birth is sufficient evidence of age. There are no seniors' cards in Argentina.

## ELECTRICITY

Argentina operates on 220V AC 50Hz. There are two types of electric plugs: those with two round prongs (as in Europe) and those with three angled, flat prongs (as in Australia and New Zealand). To use a US laptop that doesn't have a built-in 110V-to-220V converter you'll need a transformer and an adaptor. The transformer must be rated for electronic equipment – converters sold at most travel stores are for hairdryers or battery chargers and can fry your machine! Both are available at *ferreterías* (hardware stores) throughout the city.

## EMERGENCIES

As in any big city, there are rough neighborhoods in BA, and while most of the areas with tourist appeal are generally fine, they also attract pickpockets. After all, if George W Bush's daughter can have her handbag stolen in San Telmo while being protected by bodyguards, so can you! Be careful in markets and while watching tango on the streets – pickpockets love it when you're preoccupied. Walking around with a digital SLR camera screams 'rich tourist,' which makes you a more attractive target for pickpockets. While San Telmo is safe during the day, be cautious at night, and always be cautious in La Boca – take a taxi. When it comes to scams, you'll get the occasional taxi driver who'll take you for a longer ride than necessary, and there are counterfeit bank notes floating around. Don't give a taxi driver $100 unless you want to check every piece of change.

In case of an emergency:
**Ambulance** ( ☎ 107)
**Fire** ( ☎ 100)
**Police** ( ☎ 101)
**Rape crisis line** ( ☎ 4981-6882, 4958-4291)
**Tourist police** ( ☎ 4346-5748, 0800-999-5000)

## HOLIDAYS

**Año Nuevo** (New Year's Day) January 1
**Holy Thursday and Good Friday/Easter** March/April
**Día de Trabajador** (Labor Day) May 1
**Revolución de Mayo** (May Revolution) May 25
**Día de las Malvinas** (Malvinas Day) June 10
**Día de la Bandera** (Flag Day) June 20
**Día de la Independencia** (Independence Day) July 9

**Día de San Martín** (date of San Martín's death) August 17
**Día de la Raza** (Columbus Day) October 12
**Día de la Tradición** (Day of Tradition) November 10
**Día de la Concepción Inmaculada** (Immaculate Conception Day) December 8
**Navidad** (Christmas Day) December 25

## INTERNET

Throughout this book most of the websites listed are in Spanish only, but even if your Spanish is basic, most sites are easy to glean information from. Lonelyplanet .com offers speedy links to many BA websites. Other useful sites:
**Buenos Aires Herald** (www.buenosaires herald.com) Online portal of BA's English-language daily.
**Clarín** (www.clarin.com.ar, in Spanish) Argentina's largest-circulation daily.
**La Nación** (www.lanacion.com.ar, in Spanish) BA's oldest and most prestigious daily.
**Óleo** (www.guiaoleo.com, in Spanish) Extensive online guide to BA restaurants.
**Secretaría de Turismo** (www.turismo .gob.ar) The national tourist board's official Argentina website.
**Subsecretaría de Turismo** (www.bue.gov .ar) BA's official tourism website.
**What's Up Buenos Aires** (www.whatsup buenosaires.com) Tune in to what's going down in BA.

## LANGUAGE

Argentine Spanish, referred to locally as *castellano* (*rioplatense*), is heavily influenced by Italian, especially in BA. Unlike other Latin Americans, Argentines use the second-person *voseo* form (*vos* instead of *tú*). Porteño (BA local) Spanish is further complicated by Lunfardo, the slang rooted in Italian and often found in tango lyrics. Lunfardo words you'll hear include *che* (dude), *piola* (cool), *pucho* (cigarette), *morfar* (to eat) and *bondi* (bus). *Boludo* (jerk, idiot) is a favorite insult, often used in a friendly fashion. Lonely Planet's *Latin American Spanish* phrasebook is handy to have along.

### BASICS

| | |
|---|---|
| Hello. | *Hola.* |
| Goodbye. | *Adiós./Chau.* |
| Please. | *Por favor.* |
| Thank you. | *Gracias.* |
| How are you? | *¿Qué tal?* |
| I'm fine (thanks). | *Bien, gracias.* |
| Excuse me. | *Perdón.* |
| Yes. | *Sí.* |
| No. | *No.* |
| Thank you (very much). | *(Muchas) gracias.* |
| You're welcome. | *De nada./Con mucho gusto.* |
| Do you speak English? | *¿Habla inglés?* |
| I don't understand. | *No entiendo.* |
| How much is it? | *¿Cuánto vale?* |
| That's too expensive. | *Es demasiado caro.* |

### EATING & DRINKING

| | |
|---|---|
| That was delicious! | *¡Estaba buenísimo!* |

| I'm a vegetarian. | *Soy vegetariano/a.* (m/f) |
| Please bring the bill. | *La cuenta, por favor.* |

## EMERGENCIES

| I'm sick. | *Estoy enfermo/a.* (m/f) |
| Help! | *¡Socorro!* |
| Call the police! | *¡Llame a la policía!* |
| Call an ambulance! | *¡Llame a una ambulancia!* |

## DAYS & NUMBERS

| today | *hoy* |
| tonight | *esta noche* |
| tomorrow | *mañana* |

| 0 | *cero* |
| 1 | *unos* |
| 2 | *dos* |
| 3 | *tres* |
| 4 | *cautro* |
| 5 | *cinco* |
| 6 | *seis* |
| 7 | *siete* |
| 8 | *ocho* |
| 9 | *nueve* |
| 10 | *diez* |
| 11 | *once* |
| 12 | *doce* |
| 21 | *veintiuno* |
| 100 | *cien* |
| 1000 | *mil* |

## MONEY

Argentina's currency is the peso (simply denoted as $ in this book).

Bills come in denominations of two, five, 10, 20, 50 and 100 pesos. One peso equals 100 centavos; coins come in denominations of five, 10, 25 and 50 centavos, and one peso. Changing a $50 or $100 bill at kiosks or smaller businesses is nearly always impossible, so change it whenever the chance arises, and watch out for counterfeit large notes.

Leave travelers checks at home – hardly anyone accepts them. Some restaurants (even some well-known ones) don't accept credit cards, so always check first. When using credit cards at supermarkets and shopping centers, cashiers may ask for photo identification. ATMs are everywhere in BA, but they can run out of money quickly on weekends.

## NEWSPAPERS & MAGAZINES

The capital's biggest daily newspapers are *Clarín* and *La Nación;* the only English-language daily is the *Buenos Aires Herald*. For sports news, pick up *Olé*. For opinionated leftist news, pick up *Página 12*. If you're craving English magazines, apart from *Time* and *Newsweek* at some newsstands, you're pretty much out of luck.

## ORGANIZED TOURS

Fascinating architecture, neighborhood, soccer, history, art and cultural tours are available. The following tour companies have English-speaking guides – just let them know that you need one.

**BA Local** ( ☎ 4554-1877; www.balocal.com) Stylish, tailor-made excursions into BA's fashion, dining and cultural scenes with an ex-New Yorker.

**Cicerones** ( ☎ 4330-0800; www.cicerones.org.ar) A nonprofit (and free) organization that matches visitors' language needs and interests with one of its porteño volunteers.

**Eternautas** ( ☎ 4384-7874; www.eternautas.com) Thematic urban tours such as 'Evita' and 'Perónism,' plus full-day tours and excursions.

**Jewish Tours Argentina** (www.jewish-tours.com.ar) Personalized tours through the city's Jewish past with a knowledgeable local guide.

**La Bicicleta Naranja** ( ☎ 4362-1104; www.labicicletanaranja.com.ar) Bike rentals and a good range of organized bike tours.

**Tangol** ( ☎ 4312-7276; www.tangol.com) Long-standing operator offering the best fútbol (soccer) tours.

**Urban Biking** ( ☎ 4568-4321; www.urbanbiking.com) One-day cycling tours – including an alternative 'nightlife' bike trip – and bike & kayak excursions to Tigre.

## TELEPHONE

Two companies, Telecom and Telefónica, split the city's telephone services. The easiest way to make a local call is to find a locutorio (small telephone office), where you call from a private cabin and pay at the register when you're through. There's a locutorio on practically every other block – they cost about the same as street phones, are much quieter and you won't run out of coins. Most locutorios are supplied with phone books. The main cell phone systems are CDMA and TDMA. It's now possible to use a tri-band GSM world cell phone in BA, and you can buy SIM cards to use locally. If you're just here for a few days you can rent a cell phone – Tangol (left) will even deliver it and pick it up again before you leave the city.

## COUNTRY & CITY CODES

All telephone numbers in the greater Buenos Aires area have eight digits; cell phone numbers are always preceded by an extra '15.' Argentina's country code is ☎ 54, and the area code for BA (within Argentina) is ☎ 011. If calling from abroad, dial your country's code before 54 11 and the eight digits, or, if you're calling a cell phone, 54 911 and the last eight digits.

Toll-free numbers begin with ☎ 0800 or ☎ 0810.

## USEFUL PHONE NUMBERS

**Directory assistance** ( ☎ 110)
**International direct-dial code** ( ☎ 00 + country code)
**International operator** ( ☎ 000)
**Telecom/Telefónica service** ( ☎ 112)

## TIPPING

Unless the service is truly horrible, tip 10% on restaurant tabs, even when a cubierto (silverware and bread charge) is included. Bar-tenders are occasionally tipped, and they often ring a bar bell when it happens. Leave cab drivers the small change.

## TOURIST INFORMATION

The **Secretaría de Turismo de la Nación** (Map p63, B3; ☎ 4312-2232; www .turismo.gob.ar; Av Santa Fe 883, Microcentro; ☺ 9am-5pm Mon-Fri) provides information on BA and Argentina. The **Comisaría del Turista** (Map p37, C3; Tourist Police; ☎ 4346-5748, 0800-999-5000; turista@policia federal.gov.ar; Av Corrientes 436, Microcentro; ☺ 24hr) provides interpreters and helps crime victims.

Several of the city's tourist kiosks do not have telephones (or sometimes anyone who speaks English!), but there is a toll-free **tourist information line** ( ☎ 0800-555-0016; ☺ 8am-8pm). Tourist kiosk locations:

**Aeroparque airport** ( ☎ 4773-9805; ☺ 8am-8pm)

**Ezeiza airport** ( ☎ 4480-0224; ☺ 8am-8pm)

**Microcentro** (Map p37, B4; cnr Florida & Diagonal Roque Sáenz Peña, Microcentro; ☺ 9am-6pm Mon-Sat)

**Puerto Madero** (Map p47, A2; ☎ 4313-0187; Dique 4, Puerto Madero; ☺ 11am-6pm Mon-Fri, to 7pm Sat)

**Recoleta** (Map p91, E2; Av Quintana 596, Recoleta; ☺ 10:30am-6:30pm Mon-Fri, 10am-7pm Sat & Sun)

**Retiro** (Map p63, C3; Florida & Marcelo T de Alvear, Retiro; ☺ 10am-7pm)

**Retiro Bus Terminal** (Map p63, D1; ☎ 4311-0528; Ste 83, 2nd fl, Av Ramos Mejía 1680, Retiro; ☺ 7:30am-1pm Mon-Sat)

## TRAVELERS WITH DISABILITIES

Travelers with disabilities will find getting around BA difficult but not impossible. Negotiating the city's narrow, busy and uneven sidewalks in a wheelchair can be a challenge. Crossing streets can be tricky, since not every corner has ramps, and Argentine drivers have little patience. Nevertheless, Argentines with disabilities do get around, and there are a few *piso bajo* (lowered floor for wheelchair lifts) buses.

Throughout this book, listings marked with a ⓑ icon are wheelchair accessible. Every place is different, of course, but as a general guideline we have included the icon where access is relatively easy.

### INFORMATION & ORGANIZATIONS

In Buenos Aires, **Transpdisc** ( ☎ 4328-6921; www.transpdisc.com.ar) offers private transportation and day tours in vans fully equipped for wheelchair users. If you're taking a tour with another agency, Transpdisc can provide transportation alone, provided you ask your tour company to arrange it with Transpdisc.

Online, check out the following:

**Access-able Travel Source** (www.access -able.com)

**accesible.com** (www.accesible.com.ar)

**Mobility International** (www.miusa.org)

# >INDEX

*See also separate subindexes for Drink (p173), Eat (p174), Play (p174), See (p175) and Shop (p176).*

## A

Abasto 108
accommodations 136-7
    farm stays 146
afternoon tea 97
air travel 160-1
Alfonsín, Raúl 154
ambulance services 165
antiques 73-4, 75
architecture 149
art 100, 147
    festivals 24-5
    folk 72
    galleries 60, 147, *see also* See *subindex*
    street 126
arteBA 24-5
artisan fairs 15, 21, 73, 96
ATMs 167

## B

Barrio Chino 130, 133
Barrio Norte 90-101, **91**
bars 82, 142, *see also* Drink *subindex*
Basílica de Nuestra Señora del Pilar 92
beef 22, 132
Belgrano 128-33, **129**
Biblioteca Nacional 92-3
bike paths 116
billiards 59-60
boat travel 161-2

books 157
bookstores 57, 58, 95-6
Borges, Jorge Luis 68, 157
Bosques de Palermo 107
bus travel 163
business hours 164, *see also inside front cover*

## C

Cabildo de Buenos Aires 38
cafes 14, *see also* Drink *subindex*
Caminito 18, 86
canoeing 148
Carnaval 24
*cartoneros* 155
Casa de la Cultura 38
Casa FOA 26
Casa Rosada 38
Catedral Metropolitana 38
cathedrals, *see* See *subindex*
cell phones 168
Cementerio de la Recoleta 11, 93
Centro Cultural Borges 39
Centro Cultural de los Artistas 88
Centro Cultural Recoleta 93
children, travel with 65, 150
Chinatown 130, 133
Chinese New Year 24
churches, *see* See *subindex*
Ciudad Cultural Konex 108
climate change 162
clubbing 122, 143, *see also* Play *subindex*

cocktails 82, 142
Congreso 52-61, **53**
Cortázar, Julio 157
Costanera Norte 122
costs, *see inside front cover*
credit cards 167
Creamfields Buenos Aires 26
currency 167, *see also inside front cover*
cycling tours 168

## D

dance clubs 122, 143, *see also* Play *subindex*
*desaparecidos* 152
design
    exhibitions 26
    markets 15, 21, 73, 96
dinner reservations 111
disabilities, travelers with 169
drinking, *see also* Drink *subindex*
    Barrio Norte 99
    Belgrano 132
    Congreso 58-9
    Las Cañitas 132
    Microcentro 43-4
    Palermo Viejo 122-4
    Puerto Madero 50-1
    Recoleta 99
    Retiro 68-9
    San Telmo 79-82
    Tribunales 58-9

**000** map pages

drinks
  cocktails 82, 142
  *mate* 106
  tea 97
  wine 16
Duhalde, Eduardo 154

E
economy 152, 155
Edificio Kavanagh 64
El Molino 54
El Museo Fortabat 48
El Zanjón de Granados 72
electricity 165
emergencies 165, *see also inside front cover*
*empanadas* 88
environmental issues 155-6
*estancias* 146
events 23-6
exchange rates, *see inside front cover*

F
Faena Hotel + Universe 46, 50, 51, 136-7
Falkland Islands war 154
farm stay accommodations 146
fashion 145, *see also Shop subindex*
  festivals 25
Feria de Artesanos de Plaza Francia 96
Feria de Mataderos 21, 58
Feria del Libro 24
Feria San Pedro Telmo 73
Festival Internacional de Cine Independiente 24
festivals 23-6
Fiesta del Inmigrante 26
*filete* 72
film festivals 24

films 158
fire services 165
Firpo, Luis Angel 11
Floralis Genérica 94
folk art 72
folk music 19, 58, 111, 127, 158
food 141, *see also Eat subindex, Shop subindex*
  Barrio Norte 98-9
  beef 22, 132
  Belgrano 131
  Congreso 57-8
  *empanadas* 88
  ice cream 109
  La Boca 88
  Las Cañitas 131
  Microcentro 42-3
  Palermo 109-10
  Palermo Viejo 118-22
  Puerto Madero 49-50
  Recoleta 98-9
  reservations 111
  Retiro 66-8
  San Telmo 76-9
  Tribunales 57-8
free activities 31
Fundación Proa 18, 86
*fútbol* 12, 89, 148

G
Galería Güemes 39
Galerías Pacífico 40-1
galleries 60, 147, *see also See subindex*
Gardel, Carlos 25, 56, 108, 138
gardens 20, 49, 64, 72, 104, 107
gay travelers 26, 144
government 154-5
  military (1976-82) 152, 153-4

H
Hernández, José 157
Hipódromo Argentino 133
history 152-5
holidays 165
horse shows 24

I
ice cream 109
Iglesia Santa Catalina 39
internet resources 166
itineraries 29-31, 65

J
Jardín Botánico Carlos Thays 104
Jardín Japonés 104
Jardín Zoológico 104
jazz music 101, 111
jewelry, *see Shop subindex*

K
kayaking 48
Kirchner, Cristina Fernández de 152, 154, 155
Kirchner, Nestor 152, 154, 155

L
La Boca 18, 84-9, **85**
La Bombonera 12, 89
La Feria de Mataderos 21
La Rural 25, 104
La Semana del Arte en Buenos Aires 25
language 166-7
  slang 80
Las Cañitas 128-33, **129**
Las Madres de Plaza de Mayo 17, 40, 58, 152
leather 41, 66, 97, 117-8
lesbian travelers 26, 144
literature 157
Lunfardo 80

## M

Macri, Mauricio 154
magazines 167
MALBA 105
malls 40-1, 97, 107, 108, 109
Manzana de las Luces 39-40
Maradona, Diego 89
Marcha del Orgullo Gay 26
markets 15, 21, 58, 73, 74-5, 96, 130
Martín, Benito Quinquela 86, 159
Mataderos 58
*mate* 106
meat 22, 132
Ménem, Carlos 154
Mercado de San Telmo 74-5
Microcentro 36-45, **37**
military government (1976-82) 152, 153-4
*milongas* 10, 45, 60, 61, 125, 127
mobile phones 168
money 164-5, 167
Monumento a los Españoles 105
Monumento a Sarmiento 105
Museo Casa Carlos Gardel 108
Museo de Arte Español 130
Museo de Arte Popular José Hernández 105-6
Museo de Artes Plásticas Eduardo Sívori 106
Museo de Bellas Artes de la Boca Benito Quinquela Martín 86
Museo de la Inmigración 48
Museo de la Pasión Boquense 86-8

Museo Etnográfico 40
Museo Evita 106
Museo Fragata Sarmiento 48
Museo Histórico Nacional 72
Museo Municipal de Arte Hispanoamericano Isaac Fernández Blanco 64
Museo Nacional de Arte Decorativo 106-7
Museo Nacional de Bellas Artes 94
Museo Xul Solar 94
museums 147, *see also* See subindex
music 140, 158-9, *see also* Play subindex, tango festivals 26
    folk 19, 58, 111, 127, 158
    jazz 101, 111

## N

ND/Ateneo 69
newspapers 167
nightclubs 122, 143, *see also* Play subindex
Nuestros Caballos 24

## O

Obelisco 40
Once 108
opening hours 164, *see also* inside front cover

## P

Palacio Barolo 54
Palacio de las Aguas Corrientes 54
Palacio del Congreso 54
Palais de Glace 95
Palermo 102-11, **103**
Palermo Viejo 112-27, **114-15**
Palermo Woods 107
parks 20, 49, 64, 72, 104, 107

Parque 3 de Febrero 107
Parque Lezama 72
*parrillas* 22, *see also* Eat subindex
passports 162
*peñas* 19, 58, 111, 127
Perón, Eva 'Evita' 11, 93, 106, 153
Perón, Juan 153
Piazzolla, Astor 139
planning 30, 164
plastic surgery 156
Plaza de Mayo 17, 40
Plaza del Congreso 54-6
Plaza Dorrego 73
Plaza San Martín 64
police 165
politics 154-5
pollution 155-6
polo 26, 148
pride marches 26
Puerto Madero 46-51, **47**

## R

Recoleta 90-101, **91**
religion 156
*remises* 164
Reserva Ecológica Costanera Sur 49
restaurants, *see* food, Eat subindex
Retiro 62-9, **63**

## S

Sábato, Ernesto 157
San Telmo 13, 70-83, **71**
Sarmiento, Domingo 11
senior travelers 165
shopping, *see also* Shop subindex
    Barrio Norte 95-8
    Belgrano 130-1

000 map pages

Congreso 56-7
La Boca 88
Las Cañitas 130-1
malls 40-1, 97, 107, 108, 109
Microcentro 40-2
Palermo 107-9
Palermo Viejo 113-18
Recoleta 95-8
Retiro 64-6
San Telmo 73-6
Tribunales 56-7
soccer 12, 89, 148
sports 12, 89, 148
Subte 163-4
subway, see Subte

T
tango 10, 138-9
    classes 45, 60, 127
    festival 25
    Gardel, Carlos 25, 56, 108, 138
    halls 45, 60, 61, 125, 127
    shows 59-60, 82, 83
Tango Buenos Aires 25
tax 163
taxis 164
tea 97
Teatro Colón 60
Teatro Nacional Cervantes 61
Teatro San Martín 61
telephone services 168
theater 60, 61, 108, see also
    Play subindex
tipping 168-9
Torre de los Ingleses 64
tourist information 169
tours 167-8
    shopping 116
train travel 164
Tribunales 52-61, **53**

V
vacations 165
visas 162-3

W
wine 16
    festivals 25
writers' festivals 24

X
Xul Solar, Alejandro 94, 159

Y
Yrigoyen, Hipólito 11
Yupanqui, Atahulapa 159-158

Z
zoos 104

## DRINK

### Bars & Clubs

647 79
Bar 6 123
Bar Británico 79
Bar Iberia 58
Bar Plaza Dorrego 79
Bar Seddón 79
Buller Pub & Brewery 99
Caracas 123
Carnal 123
Casa Cruz 123
Clásica y Moderna 99
Cruzat Beer House 58-9
Dadá 69
Doppelgänger 80
El Federal 80
El Living 59
Gibraltar 80
Home Hotel 123-4
Kandi 131
La Cigale 43-4
La Puerta Roja 82
Le Bar 44
Lelé de Troya 124
Malas Artes 124
Marriott Plaza Bar 69
Milión 99
Mundo Bizarro 124
New Brighton 44
Pipí-Cucú 132
Puerta Uno 132
Soul Café 132
Sugar 124-5
Supersoul 132
The Library Lounge 51
Van Koning 132-3
White Bar 51

### Cafes

Bar 6 123
Bar Británico 79
Bar Iberia 58
Bar Plaza Dorrego 79
Bar Seddón 79
Café Literario Osvaldo Bayer 58
Café Retiro 68
Café Richmond 43
Café Tortoni 43
Clásica y Moderna 99
El Federal 80
La Biela 99
Las Violetas 44
L'Orangerie 97
Malas Artes 124
Mark's Deli 124
New Brighton 44
Oui Oui 124

### Gay & Lesbian Cafes

Pride Café 82

### Pubs

Bangalore Pub & Curry House 122
Buller Pub & Brewery 99
Cruzat Beer House 58-9

INDEX

# EAT

### Argentine
788 Food Bar 98
Almacén Secreto 118
Bo Bo 119
Casa Felix 118
Cocina Garden 118
Cocina Sunae 118
Cluny 119
Cumaná 98
El Federal 67
Freud y Fahler 120
La Vinería de Gualterio
  Bolívar 77
Manolo 77
Museo Evita Restaurante 109-10
Restó 57
Social Paraíso 122
Tomo 1 43
Treintasillas 118

### Asian
Cantina Chinatown 133
Comedor Nikkai 76-7
Empire Thai 67
Green Bamboo 120
Little Rose 121
Lotus Neo Thai 133
Moshi Moshi 131
Sipan 68
Sudestada 122

### Delis
i Fresh Market 50-1
Matilda's Café 77-8

### European
Cluny 119
Ølsen 121

### French
Azema Exotic Bistró 118
Brasserie Berry 42
Brasserie Petanque 76
Casa Roca 42
La Bourgogne 98
Le Sud 68

### International
Azema Exotic Bistró 118
California Burrito Company 42
El Mercado 50
Gran Bar Danzon 98
La Fábrica del Taco 121
Novecento 131-2
Tea Connection 110

### Italian
Amici Miei 76
D'Oro 42-3
El Cuartito 57
Filo 67-8
Il Ballo del Mattone 120
Il Matterello 88
La Parolaccia del Mare 51

### Middle Eastern
Sarkis 121

### Organic
Origen 78
Pura Vida 43

### Parrillas
Cabaña Las Lilas 49
Don Julio 120
El Desnivel 77
El Establo 66-7
El Obrero 88
Gran Parrilla del Plata 77
La Dorita 120-1
Miranda 121
Parrilla 1880 78

### Peruvian
Sipan 68
Status 57-8

### Seafood
Plaza Asturias 57

### Spanish & Basque
Café San Juan 76
La Vinería de Gualterio
  Bolívar 77
Oviedo 99
Plaza Asturias 57
Sagardi Euskal Taberna 78-9
Taberna Baska 79

### Vegetarian
Artemisia 109
Bio 118-19
Pura Vida 43

# PLAY

### Concert & Live Music Venues
Centro Cultural Torquato
  Tasso 82
Ciudad Cultural Konex
  108
La Cumparsita 83
La Peña del Colorado 111
La Trastienda 83
Los Cardones 127
Luna Park 45
ND/Ateneo 69
Niceto Club 127
Notorious 101
Teatro Gran Rex 45
Thelonious Club 111

### Dance Clubs
Asia de Cuba 51
Bahrein 44-5

**000** map pages

Basement Club 101
Big One 45
Caix 122
Club Aráoz 110
Cocoliche 45
Crobar 110-11
Jet 122
Maluco Beleza 60
Mandarine 122
Museum 83
Niceto Club 127
Pachá 122
Rouge 122

Gay & Lesbian Bars & Clubs
Bach Bar 125
Bulnes Class 110
Glam 101
Sitges 127

Jazz Clubs
Notorious 101
Thelonious Club 111

Sporting Venues
Campo Argentino de Polo de
    Palermo 132
Hipódromo Argentino 133
La Bombonera 12, 89

Tango
36 Billares 59
Bar Sur 82
Centro Cultural Torquato
    Tasso 82
Centro Region Leonesa 61
Confitería Ideal 45
El Beso 60
El Querandí 83
El Viejo Almacén 83
La Cumparsita 83
La Viruta 125
Salon Canning 127

Theater
Ciudad Cultural Konex 108
Teatro Colón 60
Teatro Nacional Cervantes 61
Teatro San Martín 61

## SEE

Churches & Cathedrals
Basílica de Nuestra Señora
    del Pilar 92
Catedral Metropolitana 38
Iglesia Santa Catalina 39

Museums & Galleries
Braga Menendez Arte
    Contemporaneo 60
Casa de la Cultura 38
Centro Cultural Borges 39
Centro Cultural Recoleta 93
Daniel Abate 94
El Museo Fortabat 48
Floralis Genérica 94
Fundación Proa 86
Isabel Anchorena 94
MALBA 105
Museo Casa Carlos Gardel 108
Museo de Arte Español 130
Museo de Arte Popular José
    Hernández 105-6
Museo de Artes Plásticas
    Eduardo Sívori 106
Museo de Bellas Artes de
    la Boca Benito Quinquela
    Martín 86
Museo de la Inmigración 48
Museo de la Pasión Boquense
    86-8
Museo Etnográfico 40
Museo Evita 106
Museo Fragata Sarmiento 48
Museo Histórico Nacional 72

Museo Municipal de Arte
    Hispanoamericano Isaac
    Fernández Blanco 64
Museo Nacional de Arte
    Decorativo 106-7
Museo Nacional de Bellas
    Artes 94
Museo Xul Solar 94
Ruth Benzacar 60
Zavaleta Lab 60

Notable Buildings &
Monuments
Biblioteca Nacional 92-3
Cabildo de Buenos Aires 38
Casa Rosada 38
Cementerio de la Recoleta
    11, 93
Edificio Kavanagh 64
El Molino 54
El Zanjón de Granados 72
Galería Güemes 39
Manzana de las Luces 39-40
Monumento a los Españoles 105
Monumento a Sarmiento 105
Obelisco 40
Palacio Barolo 54
Palacio de las Aguas
    Corrientes 54
Palacio del Congreso 54
Palais de Glace 95
Puente de la Mujer 48-9
Torre de los Ingleses 64

Parks & Gardens
Jardín Botánico Carlos Thays 104
Jardín Japonés 104
Parque 3 de Febrero 107
Parque Lezama 72
Plaza San Martín 64
Reserva Ecológica Costanera
    Sur 49

**Plazas & Streets**
Barrio Chino 130
Caminito 18, 86
Plaza de Mayo 40
Plaza del Congreso 54-6
Plaza Dorrego 73

**Zoos**
Jardín Zoológico 104

## 🏠 SHOP

**Antiques**
El Buen Orden 73
Gabriel del Campo Anticuario 74
Gil Antigüedades 73-4
HB Antiques 74
Imhotep 74
Mercado de San Telmo 74-5

**Art**
Autoría 64
Centro Cultural de los Artistas 88

**Books & Music**
Café Literario Osvaldo Bayer 58
El Ateneo Grand Splendid 95-6
Gandhi Galerna 57
Walrus Books 76

**Fashion**
A.Y. Not Dead 95
Calma Chicha 113
Cora Groppo 113-16
DAM 116
El Buen Orden 73
Felix 116
Gil Antigüedades 73-4
Hermanos Estebecorena 117
Jeans Makers 109

Juana de Arco 117
Moebius 75
Nadine Zlotogora 117
Pablo Ramírez 75
Puntos en el Espacio 75
Rapsodia 118
Tramando 97

**Food & Wine**
0800-Vino 108
Anuva Vinos 130
El Fenix 96
Ligier 66
Lo de Joaquin Alberdi 117
Ruffino Bazar & Vinos 75-6
Tealosophy 97
Valenti 130
Winery 42

**Home Decor**
airedelsur 95
Autoría 64
Buenos Aires Design 95
Calma Chicha 113
L'Ago 74
Materia Urbana 74
Tramando 97

**Jewelry**
JCB Gems & Carvings 66
Plata Nativa 41

**Leather**
Casa Lopez 66
El Remanso 66
Humawaca 117
Prüne 41
Rossi & Caruso 97

**Malls**
Alto Palermo 107
El Abasto 108
Galerías Pacífico 40-1
Paseo Alcorta 109
Patio Bullrich 97

**Markets**
Feria de Artesanos de Plaza Francia 96
Feria de Mataderos 58
Feria Modelo de Belgrano 130
Feria San Pedro Telmo 73
Mercado de San Telmo 74-5

**Shoes**
28 Sport 113
Corre Lola 116
Darcos Tango 40
Josefina Ferroni 96-7
Puntos en el Espacio 75

**Souvenirs & Handicrafts**
airedelsur 95
Arte de Pueblos 56
Artesanos de Argentina 73
Centro Cultural de los Artistas 88
Club de Tango 56
Darcos Tango 40
Fundación Silataj 130
JCB Gems & Carvings 66
L'Ago 74
Papelera Palermo 117-18
Plata Nativa 41
Tierra Adentro 66
Wussmann Shop 97-8